BUILDING BETTER ARMIES:
AN INSIDER'S ACCOUNT OF LIBERIA

INTRODUCTION

In March 2012, a group of mutinying Malian soldiers staged a coup that overthrew that nation's constitutionally-elected government and attacked the presidential palace, state television, and military barracks. Soon after, mayhem followed. As the international community condemned the coup, the Taureg rebellion seized northern Mali and threatened to advance south, fuelled by small arms from Libya and al-Qaeda affiliates. Timbuktu and other towns in the north fell to the advancing rebels, and a strict version of Islamic law was imposed. Finally, the French intervened with military force and pushed the rebels out of the area.

One disturbing story to this saga is the fact that the United States had been training the Malian armed forces for a number of years, including Captain Amadou Sanogo, who led the military coup. Reports indicate that Malian soldiers were overrun by rebels and even defected to the enemy side. General Carter F. Ham, commander of U.S. Africa Command (AFRICOM), summed it up best: "[This is] very worrisome for us."[1]

Nor is this worry limited to Africa. In 2012, one in seven of all North Atlantic Treaty Organization (NATO) deaths in Afghanistan were at the hands of the very Afghan troops the coalition was training.[2] These "green on blue" attacks describe an alarming series of incidents where seemingly rogue Afghan security forces turn their guns on their NATO counterparts. In order to prevent further attacks, NATO responded in

September 2012 by halting joint operations with Afghan security forces, following the deaths of six International Security Assistance Force (ISAF) troops over 1 weekend. A bleak Pentagon report found that only one of the Afghan National Army's 23 brigades was able to operate independently without air or other military support from the United States and NATO partners.[3] This does not augur well for the Afghan security forces' ability to take over after the United States withdraws in 2014, leaving a security vacuum in a volatile region. U.S. efforts in Iraq have been similarly frustrated as have United Nations' (UN) experiences in the Balkans, Haiti, Timor-Leste, and the Democratic Republic of the Congo. This bodes poorly for potential efforts in Syria and Libya.

Helping allies build better armies and police forces is a strategic imperative. Operationally, building professional indigenous security forces is the exit strategy for costly stability operations like Afghanistan because it allows those countries to provide security for themselves rather than depend on the United States to do so. Strategically, helping fragile states professionalize their military and police promotes durable development, since corrupt security forces tend to devour the fruits of development. Additionally, the United States must help its partners develop effective security forces to contend with regional and transnational threats, or it will face a Hobson's choice: Send in U.S. troops to do the job or permit minor threats to fester into major ones.

Despite this strategic imperative, recent events in Mali, Libya, Afghanistan, Iraq, and elsewhere demonstrate that few success stories exist. There are numerous reasons for this: It is hard to do; there is a theory to practice gap on how to do it; there are no comprehensive practitioner guides or field manuals; and few practical models exist. The current "train and equip" model is ineffective, as it focuses too much on tactics and techniques and misses the important intangibles. Or as General Ham reflected after Mali: "We didn't spend, probably, the requisite time focusing on values, ethics, and military ethos."[4]

One alternate model and qualified success is Liberia. Ten years ago, it was one of the world's worst post-conflict zones, and now its military is deploying to Mali in the peacekeeping mission. This is a remarkable transformation, given the fact that Liberian President Charles Taylor used much of the Liberian military as an instrument of terror. In 2012, the UN-backed Special Court for Sierra Leone at The Hague sentenced him to 50 years in prison for war crimes. Today, the military is seen as a relative success, and the program that built it is unique and unlike those in Iraq and Afghanistan, making it a good case study.

This monograph explains how the Liberian armed forces were transformed from a weapon of terror into an instrument of security by one who helped design and implement this *sui generis* program. Whether one is raising an army of 2,000 or 200,000, the methods are essentially the same, differing only in scale and scope. The two tools needed to help a country acquire the monopoly of legitimate force are disarmament, demobilization, and reintegration (DDR) and security sector reform (SSR). This monograph explores the theory and practice behind these two programs, using the case of Liberia where national forces were complicit in atrocities and human rights abuses.

The United States must develop a solid capability to build better armies, or it will remain mired in conflict affected countries like Afghanistan, face strategic surprises in places like Mali, and be powerless to prepare the future in countries like Libya and Syria. Helping allies help themselves is a force multiplier and a core pillar of U.S. national security strategy.

ESTABLISHING A STATE'S MONOPOLY OF FORCE

A state requires the monopoly of force within its territorial boundaries in order to uphold its rule of law and promote stability. However, the challenges of this are daunting in conflict affected countries because armed groups are the de facto institutions of power, and any attempt to alter them is deeply political. It is also dangerous. Convincing a general or warlord to put down his weapons and become a farmer may not be welcomed and may even provoke violence. In 2002, the government of neighboring Côte d'Ivoire attempted to demobilize 750 soldiers, who, in response, staged a coup leading to a civil war that lasted for several years, despite a French and UN armed intervention to maintain peace. These programs are extremely political, and technical approaches alone court catastrophe.

Technically, the methods and processes for building effective indigenous security forces are the same for both small and large countries; they are DDR and SSR. DDR consolidates the state's monopoly of force by disbanding the competition, such as militias and insurgents, who threaten the country's ability to impose its governance. SSR professionalizes and strengthens the state's statutory armed actors so that they can responsibly enforce the law of the land and defend it from armed threats.

4

In theory, DDR and SSR work together in tandem to help uphold the state's rule of law and are also gateway capacities, since security, law and order are prerequisites of sustainable development and overall stability. However, in practice, this is rarely done because DDR and SSR are difficult and dangerous. For example, in Liberia the state forces themselves were complicit in wide-scale atrocities and human rights abuses. How exactly does one transform the military from a symbol of terror into an instrument of democracy? How can one make a soldier someone a child would run toward for safety rather than away from in fear?

DDR: Disbanding the Competition.

The first step in establishing a state's monopoly of force is disbanding the competition. This means disarming, demobilizing, and reintegrating combatants safely into civil society and enabling them to earn livelihoods through peaceful means.[5] DDR is the fulcrum between war and peace. In the short term, those who do not find peaceful ways to make a living are likely to return to conflict or join gangs; in the long term, disaffected ex-combatants can challenge public order and polarize political debate, since they are often easy targets of populist, reactionary, and extremist movements. To date, the UN is the leader in developing and implementing DDR, with programs in Burundi, Côte d'Ivoire, Democratic Republic of Congo, Liberia, Sierra Leone, Sudan, Uganda, Afghanistan, Nepal, the Solomon Islands, and Haiti.[6]

As the term implies, DDR is a three-stage process. The first stage involves disarming combatants, who report to a safe and secure cantonment site within the conflict zone to turn in their small arms, munitions, and light and heavy weapons. This is usually linked to a broader small arms and light weapons counter-proliferation program that documents and destroys the weapons and munitions. The second stage demobilizes and disbands the armed nonstate groups, formally breaking up command structures and marking their official entry into civilian life. Lastly, ex-combatants are reintegrated into civil society to prevent another escalation of conflict. This typically is divided into two parts: initial rehabilitation and long-term reintegration. Initial rehabilitation entails giving ex-combatants short-term support packages and transporting them back to their homes to begin their new lives. Long-term reintegration involves job training and placement programs, working with communities to accept ex-combatants and monitoring progress in the difficult transition to civilian life. The overall goal of DDR is to ensure permanent demobilization and sustainable peace.

DDR is fraught with operational challenges that can quickly backfire, possibly fomenting armed conflict. First, combatants often do not relinquish their weapons if they do not believe the peacekeeping force can ensure their safety. Owing to this, the peacekeeping force must be large enough to monopolize force and to be perceived as credibly neutral by all parties, which is tricky in a post-conflict country where distrust is ubiquitous. Second, armed groups generally hold back their best fighters and weapons as a hedge against others who renege on the peace agreement. This creates a prisoner's dilemma that encourages preemptive defections from the peace process, as rebel groups fear that rivals will defect first and gain the advantage of surprise in a renewed war.[7] Mismanagement of a DDR process—which is easy to do—creates a classic race to the bottom.

Third, a combatant group typically disarms only if all combatants disarm; otherwise, the disarmed are vulnerable to the armed, who may seek reprisal or gain against their defenseless enemies. Although simple in theory, simultaneously disarming tens of thousands of combatants in a highly chaotic and dangerous failed state with little logistical infrastructure and much unresolved bad blood is thorny in practice. Fourth, the victims of violence may not welcome DDR, as they may question why the worst actors in the war are rewarded with money and jobs, while the innocent get little or nothing—even if failing to transition combatants to civilian life almost guarantees more violence and victims.

Lastly, a DDR process requires a reliable funding source. A program that runs out of money halfway through can be worse than no program at all, since a temporary or premature shutdown may provoke an attack by the armed on the unarmed or encourage ex-combatants to take up the gun again to make a living. Also, ex-combatants who are denied benefits might seek reprisals against DDR staff. Unfortunately, it is difficult to forecast DDR funding needs in conflicts like that in Liberia, where nearly everyone is a perpetrator of violence, a victim, or both.

Owing to this, many DDR programs prioritize the *DD* to get the guns and gangs off the streets but leave the *R* to wither. The problem of the forgotten *R*—that is, not fully reintegrating ex-combatants into society—involves them turning rogue again, perpetuating the cycle of violence as they earn a living or gain status through violent crime. This manifests itself most visibly in criminal gangs, which often form from demobilized groups and can terrorize the population, hinder peace efforts, and challenge the new police and army's legitimacy. Worse, unlike combatant groups, gangs cannot undergo DDR because they are a law enforcement problem and must be arrested, tried, and incarcerated within the criminal justice system.[8] In a failed state, this adds a layer of complexity to an already complex situation.

In Liberia, the UN and United States shared DDR responsibilities. The UN conducted the bulk of DDR as it disarmed the entire country and demobilized and reintegrated nonstate armed actors, such as Liberians United for Reconciliation and Democracy (LURD) and the Movement for Democracy in Liberia (MODEL), as well as Liberian law enforcement. The United States demobilized and reintegrated the Armed Forces of Liberia (AFL). According to the UN, it disarmed and demobilized 101,495 combatants and received 28,314 weapons and 6,486,136 rounds of small arms ammunition. Despite these numbers, the UN suffered setbacks, which is not surprising given the plethora of problems associated with DDR in failed states. There was a great deal of corruption and fraud regarding qualification for DDR benefits, resulting in incredibly high numbers of ex-combatants; many observers believe the number of actual combatants was closer to 38,000.[9]

Detractors also argue that the UN Mission in Liberia (UNMIL) began its program prematurely, in December 2003, before sufficient peacekeepers were on the ground to guarantee security. Serious riots erupted at the start of the program at Camp Schefflin, a DDR site just outside of Monrovia, and the camp was shut down. The riots were a planned attempt to disrupt UN efforts and create instability, largely to increase monetary profits for warring factions, and would have happened whenever the DDR program began.[10] Four months later, however, the program resumed without incident and remains one of the most comprehensive programs of its kind.

SSR: Acquiring the Monopoly of Force.

Working in tandem with DDR, SSR institutes the monopoly of force within a territory and enables the authority—government or otherwise—to enforce its rule of law. Broadly speaking, the "security sector" refers to those organizations and institutions that safeguard the state and its citizens from security threats. SSR is the complex task of transforming the security sector into a professional, effective, legitimate, apolitical, and accountable sector that supports the rule of law. Like DDR, SSR is deeply political, and technical approaches alone will fail. Program failure risks coup d'etat, war, or worse.

To date, creating truly successful SSR programs remains a major unmet challenge for the international community, despite the growing prevalence of peacekeeping missions and nation building around the world. There are several reasons for this. SSR is difficult to do. Also, there remains a significant theory to practice gap.[11] Consequently, there is no practicable doctrine, best practice, or even common terminology.[12] The concept itself has no commonly accepted definition and has many names: security and justice reform, security sector governance, security sector development, security force assistance, foreign internal defense, and security system transformation. As efforts to re-establish the security sectors in Iraq, Afghanistan, and elsewhere illustrate, few practical models for SSR have been developed, perpetuating cycles of violence in fragile states and prolonging costly peacekeeping missions.

While recognizing that many terms for SSR exist and connote subtle differences to academics, the basic purpose of the program remains the same to the practitioner: the reconstitution of a professional security sector that upholds the rule of law. However, before an explanation of what SSR is and how to do it, a few caveats are necessary. First, security in this context means "hard security": physically protecting citizens and the state from threats that endanger normal life, public safety and survival. The development community has created a variety of "soft security" categories, such as food security and energy security. While lack of food and energy may be contributing factors to armed conflict, SSR should not attempt to rectify food shortages or energy blackouts: That would be an overreach of program scope. For an SSR program to be manageable on the ground, it must be limited to the security sector: those public organizations and government agencies with the primary mission of providing security such as the military and police. SSR seeks to transform these organizations and institutions into professional, effective, legitimate, apolitical, and accountable actors that support the rule of law.

A second caveat is that although SSR seeks to uphold the rule of law, it should not be confused with justice sector reform (JSR). These two programs are interdependent and mutually reinforcing, but entail distinctly separate skill sets, tasks, and objectives. For example, an SSR program should not attempt to rewrite a country's constitution, address past human rights abuses and crimes against humanity, or integrate indigenous systems of justice with international norms. Nor should a JSR program attempt to recruit and train military and police forces, determine weaponry and organizational structure of security forces, or draft the national security strategy. Despite this, theorists frequently merge JSR and SSR, which can lead to operational confusion on the ground for practitioners. Such an all-encompassing program would likely result in failure owing to a mismatch of ends, ways, and means across programs.[13]

That said, an SSR program operating without a corresponding JSR program will likely be unsuccessful. Without a functioning judiciary and appropriate laws to enforce, police functionality and legitimacy suffer; officers can end up being stooges of a corrupt legal system. Similarly, a JSR program operating without a commensurate SSR effort will probably fail because criminal justice systems require professional police, prisons, customs, and other instruments of law enforcement. SSR and JSR rise and fall together: Though operationally distinct, they should be conceptually integrated and closely coordinated.

A third caveat is that SSR is more than a "train and equip" program, which, though necessary, only creates better-dressed soldiers who shoot straighter. SSR is more comprehensive than traditional train and equip programs since SSR encompasses creating new institutions, facilitating force structure[14] decisions, formulating national security strategy and doctrine, recruiting and vetting new forces, constructing military bases and road infrastructure, selecting leadership, establishing oversight mechanisms within ministries and parliament, and many other complex tasks that go well beyond simply training and equipping troops. A train and equip campaign will not transform a security sector, and such programs alone will invite failure.

The security sector itself consists of three types of actors: operational, institutional, and oversight. *Operational actors* interact directly with the public on security matters and may include law enforcement, military and paramilitary forces, border control, customs, immigration, coast guard, and intelligence services. *Institutional actors* manage the policy, programs, resources, and general administration of operational actors and may include ministries of defense, interior, and justice. *Oversight bodies* monitor and supervise the security sector; they are ideally civilian led, democratically accountable to citizens, and able to ensure that the security sector serves the people and not vice versa. Oversight bodies may include the executive, legislative, and judicial branches of government as well as municipal and district authorities. One may conceptualize the security sector as a pyramid of actors (see Figure 1). Not included in the security sector are non-statutory security forces — that is, liberation armies, armed criminal gangs, guerrilla forces, insurgents, and political party militias.

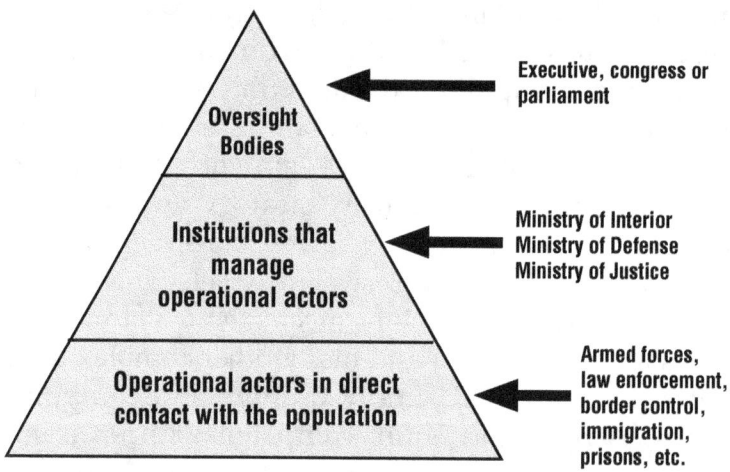

Figure 1. Taxonomy of the Security Sector.

These three types of actors can, in turn, be grouped into security sub-sectors, distinguished from one another by unique objectives, technical knowledge, capabilities, best practices, institutional culture, and professional ethos. Sub-sectors can overlap and vary widely among countries and regimes, but the idea is useful to the practitioner designing and managing an SSR program. Taken together, the hierarchy of actors and security sub-sectors form a matrix of the security sector (see Table 1).

Security Sub-Sector	Operational Actors	Institutional Actors	Oversight Actors
Military	Military, civil defense forces, national guards, militias, paramilitary	Ministry of Defense	Executive, Legislative, Parliament
Law Enforcement	Police, gendarmerie, prison, criminal justice, presidential guard	Ministry of Interior, Ministry of Justice	Executive, Legislative, Parliament, Judiciary, Municipal and District Governments and Councils
Border Management	Border control, immigration, coast guard, customs authorities	Ministry of Interior, Ministry of Defense	
Foreign Relations	Embassies, attachés, and security liaison officers	Ministry of Foreign Affairs, Ministry of Defense	Executive, Legislative, Parliament
Intelligence	Collection assets	Intelligence agencies	

Table 1. Analytical Framework of the Security Sector.[15]

This analytical framework will assist the planner categorize and understand the myriad elements of the security sector in any given country or governed area. This will also help the planner to task organize a tailored response for the SSR program. For example, if the U.S. Government is facilitating the program, it makes sense that the U.S. Department of Defense (DoD) would manage the military sub-sector among the operational and perhaps the institutional actors. Another organization like the National Democratic Institute (NDI) might work with the host nation's parliament to establish viable oversight mechanisms. As the matrix suggests, building sub-sector capacity and professionalizing actors makes SSR a fundamentally "whole of government" and comprehensive effort, making it complicated to execute.

There are several challenges to implementing SSR programs. First, though there is a growing consensus that early local ownership of SSR work is a critical component of its sustainability; translating this principle into concrete reality remains a challenge.[16] Even the definition of local ownership is contested. Deciding which local leaders and political groups truly represent local aspirations may be difficult, fraught with uncertainty, and have political ramifications in both indigenous and international politics. Also, local actors often have competing visions and priorities; choosing local partners can be perilous in conflict-affected countries where there is often imperfect knowledge of parochial agendas. In addition, it may prove difficult to keep insurgents and spoilers out of the process. If they are deemed key stakeholders, they gain legitimacy and the ability to obstruct progress from within. Finally, measuring ownership is difficult. What metrics are appropriate? Should they privilege local or international values and priorities? Local ownership is sound in theory but ambiguous in practice.

Second, as the security sector is comprised of various agencies and departments, successful SSR conceptually demands a whole of government response from donor nations. There are several reasons why this is seldom, if ever, done in practice. SSR is a relatively new idea, emerging after the Cold War, and consequently suffers from a dearth of coherent frameworks, common definitions, and technical expertise. On the practical level, SSR strategy demands cooperation from a wide range of agencies that often have conflicting perspectives, priorities, and objectives. The result is often competition between agencies and the uncoordinated and ad hoc implementation of SSR programs. Additionally, the lengthy time horizon for SSR to produce noticeable change may cause donors to lose interest or focus.

Third, SSR is a political process that must be accomplished in partnership with the country undergoing the reform. Conflict-affected countries' security forces, both statutory and nonstatutory, are the de facto institutions of power when the process begins, and altering them can provoke violent reactions and a relapse into armed conflict. It is difficult to persuade a general or warlord in Afghanistan or Liberia to put down the rifle and become a wheat farmer. International organizations or bilateral partners who ignore the political nuances of SSR and attempt to implement it in a purely unilateral and technical manner will fail.

Fourth, SSR is difficult to operationalize. The majority of countries undergoing SSR are fragile or failed states emerging from armed conflicts. Operating in wrecked countries with ruined infrastructure and in areas where everything seems to be a priority is challenging. SSR processes are resource intensive, requiring significant numbers of trainers and staff, a large logistical footprint, and a programmatic robustness capable of training, equipping, fielding, and sustaining the new security force. It takes years and even decades to create a viable security sector.

Fifth, SSR programs have few good metrics for success. Even the definition of security is ambiguous. Does it refer to state security, regional security, or human security? If all three, how should they be prioritized and integrated? Many of the principles that inform different ideas about security may not easily translate into a coherent and actionable national security strategy. The human security perspective holds that a country is secure when individuals attain "freedom from want" and "freedom from fear." How exactly should the armed forces and other instruments of national power provide this? [17]

Finally, international donors are quick to resort to traditional train-and-equip programs in an effort to improve the operational effectiveness of local security forces and put new police on the streets and soldiers in the field. Such programs quickly produce visible results and clear statistics, including the number of trainees, uniformed personnel on duty, and operational vehicles. They do little, however, to transform institutions, establish government oversight, and create an appropriate civil-military relationship, which are the goals of SSR.

Despite the challenges, SSR processes are an invaluable support for countries looking to move beyond conflict. They help the state consolidate the monopoly of force it needs to uphold the rule of law by assessing the current security sector in terms of capacity, efficiency, and relevance, and by supporting the creation of a balanced and effective security sector, informed by a clear understanding of its objectives, threats, and resources available. SSR work can reconstitute and professionalize security forces, such as the military and police; build civilian-led security-sector institutions, such as the ministries of interior, defense, and justice, which can manage security organs competently; and establish transparent oversight mechanisms for the security sector in the executive and legislative branches, providing capable security sector governance and making the security sector accountable to citizens through democracy. Finally, SSR processes can assist in developing a national security strategy that addresses the root causes of armed conflict and geopolitical threats as appropriate for that country, and translate national strategies down to local levels.

However, SSR work must itself be part of a larger peacemaking effort. It cannot resolve ongoing armed conflicts or substitute for peace enforcement activities when those are required. Nor can it address past abuse and injustices or transform the justice sector; that is, managing transitional justice, writing laws, or redressing past security-sector crimes. Finally, it cannot transition combatants to civilian life—which is the province of DDR.

DDR and SSR Linkages.

DDR and SSR should be naturally linked programs since they rise or fall together. DDR, encompassing the processes that safely transition combatants back to civilian life, and SSR, involving the reconstitution and professionalization of security institutions and actors, are interdependent and mutually reinforcing. Working in tandem, they can enable countries emerging from conflict to provide for their own security and uphold the rule of law, an essential precondition of sustainable development and part of the exit strategy for costly peacekeeping missions. As such, politically, they rise or fall together. Without a monopoly on the use of force, a state has few ways to uphold the rule of law and protect citizens from threats.[18] By definition, conflict-affected states have lost this monopoly, and the joint purpose of DDR and SSR programs is to restore or establish it by disbanding nonstate armed actors and reconstituting statutory forces.

Beyond their shared political objectives, DDR and SSR are programmatically linked, as failure of one risks failure of the other. Ex-combatants who are not properly reintegrated into civil society through DDR can complicate and potentially compromise SSR. Ex-combatants who do not successfully transition to civilian life may take up arms again or form criminal gangs, challenging newly created security institutions and forces that may lack sufficient capacity to control such threats. As the population thus becomes vulnerable to violence, the state's inability to protect its citizens undermines its legitimacy.

Inversely, if DDR succeeds but SSR falters, then people begin to rely on nonstate actors—ethnicity- or religion-based militias or village self-defense forces—for their security. In some parts of Afghanistan where the reach of national law enforcement is limited, Afghans have turned to tribal authorities or the Taliban to provide security and justice. Worse, such states can offer safe havens for armed opposition groups, insurgents, organized crime, and other armed nonstate actors that foment conflict and regional destabilization. Providing security is an essential component of governance, and states that cannot provide it are seen as inept and illegitimate.

DDR and SSR are also operationally linked, as many ex-combatants seek employment in the new security forces that SSR programs create. This transference from DDR to SSR occurs during the reintegration phase of DDR, making it the natural point of intersection between the two. That is, after being disarmed and demobilized, many ex-combatants may seek job training and reintegration in the new security sector as soldiers or policemen. They then fall under the SSR program, which vets them for past human rights abuses and assesses their qualifications for duty. No ex-combatant should ever be guaranteed a job in the new security sector without undergoing proper selection processes.

Combining DDR and SSR, if done properly, reenforces the peace settlement by fortifying mutual trust among former enemies and encouraging followers to lay down their guns and enter civilian life. This is particularly true if ex-combatants perceive that they will have a substantive role in crafting and serving in the new government. If not done properly, many will seek employment in militias, organized crime, or private security companies, allowing them to legally carry weapons. This can result in reconstituted warring parties under new names—some of which will be licensed to employ lethal force.

Lastly, DDR and SSR jointly promote development, as economic growth depends on long-term security and stability, which DDR and SSR both provide when implemented correctly. This peace dividend manifests itself in preserving resources and infrastructure, freeing and managing labor, and furthering reconciliation that encourages investment and entrepreneurship. DDR and SSR processes also promote the interests of women, minorities, and child soldiers, who should be supported in a consistent manner within the two programs. A growing body of literature illuminates the strengths of considering gender in DDR and SSR, particularly if the programs are managed together so women can benefit from and contribute to both.[19]

Despite the fundamental linkages between DDR and SSR programs, they are often planned and executed disjointedly in the field, causing problems. It has been argued, in both the academic literature and manuals for practitioners, that DDR and SSR are separate and distinct processes involving different actors, priorities, timelines, and functions. The majority of scholarship on the topic deals with either DDR or SSR but rarely treats both in an integrated manner, resulting in disjointed approaches and mismatched conceptual frameworks on reestablishing the state's monopoly of force.[20] Practioner's guides for field use tend to specialize in either one or the other but not both. For example, the UN, a leader in conducting DDR, issues DDR standards in relative isolation from SSR concerns. Similarly, the Organization for Economic Cooperation and Development-Development Assistance Committee (OECD-DAC) issues a *Handbook on Security System Reform* that does not substantially address DDR.[21] Both academia and practice generally assume DDR and SSR are separate and isolated programs, and that DDR is a relatively quick process followed sequentially by SSR, which plays out over time.

Operationally, there are serious challenges to integrating them. There are several reasons for this. First, DDR and SSR programs are political, and changing power structures in a conflict-affected country is complex and dangerous. Reintegrating ex-combatants who may still harbor legitimate grievances against the government, or transforming security institutions into those that will lawfully use force, is understandably difficult and can easily provoke a relapse into armed conflict. The political concerns, priorities, and agendas of ex-combatants in DDR versus SSR processes may differ, making it challenging for program planners to adopt a unified approach to political issues.

Different levels of local support and ownership may exist for DDR versus SSR. A population traumatized by civil war may welcome the disarming of combatants, but may shun their inclusion in new security forces, especially if distrust of the police and military linger because of atrocities committed in the past. Conversely, local populations may not welcome ex-combatants into their communities, but strongly desire a new, professional police force. These different levels of local support can decouple DDR and SSR.

Programmatically, DDR and SSR can be difficult to synchronize, owing to their differing priorities, objectives, and time horizons. DDR is complicated in that it is difficult, yet it has clear and achievable objectives, and a solution can be engineered. SSR, meanwhile, is complex in that there are no clear and achievable objectives that can reliably be measured, and a solution may not be obvious at first. Also, SSR programs take years and even decades to complete, while DDR generally takes months.

Such a separation of functions, however, has deleterious effects on the ability of conflict-affected countries to recover and establish a viable security sector. Owing to their natural linkages, and in partnership with the host nation, DDR and SSR should be planned, resourced, implemented, and evaluated as a single entity. This involves several challenges, however, both in SSR and DDR as components, and in combining them as part of a larger process.

Therefore, embedding DDR within SSR and fully integrating the two programs is the best way to deal with these challenges, and as mentioned previously, the two processes even have a natural point of intersection: the reintegration phase of DDR programs, which can flow into longer-term SSR work as ex-combatants find legal and peaceful employment in the new security apparatus that SSR programs create. Problematically, however, reintegration is also often the most difficult aspect of DDR, owing to the aforementioned issue of the forgotten R. This makes reintegration both the best place to incorporate DDR into SSR and one of the clear sites where such an incorporation can fail.

THE CASE OF LIBERIA

Monrovia is the capital of Liberia, a small West African country that, by the summer of 2003, had suffered 14 years of civil war epitomized by torture, rape, child soldiers, blood diamonds, and fratricide. The city is situated on the Atlantic Ocean and inhabits a peninsula parallel to the mainland with only three entrances: one road and two bridges. On July 18, 2003, the city was sealed off by rebels—from the east by LURD and from the south by MODEL. Ferociously defending the gateways to Monrovia were remnants of the AFL still loyal to President Taylor, a notorious warlord accused of war crimes and crimes against humanity.[22] At the time, Liberia was more of a kingdom than a state. As one Liberian put it, "Ghankay [Charles Taylor] is our law. He understands that the man with the gun is a strongman."[23]

Taylor has been accused of murdering and mutilating civilians during his reign from 1989 to 2003, illegally trafficking in diamonds and timber to enrich himself at the expense of the state, abducting women and girls as sex slaves, and forcing children and adults into pressed labor and fighting during the war in Sierra Leone.[24] His militias chased down civilians and asked them if they wanted a long-sleeved or a short-sleeved shirt. For people who said long sleeves, the fighters hacked off their hands at the wrist with a machete. People who said short sleeves had their arms hacked off closer to the shoulder. To this day, people missing one, two, and even four limbs lie on the streets of Monrovia begging for money.[25] Taylor also supported rebel groups in the adjacent countries of Guinea and Côte d'Ivoire to agitate ongoing conflicts there and destabilize his neighbors. In July 2003, those same countries returned the favor, helping unseat Taylor by aiding LURD and MODEL. In late 2002, *The Economist* predicted that Liberia would be "the world's worst place to live" that year.[26] They were right.

The fighting was fierce, and all sides committed atrocities. Child soldiers were commonplace, the line between combatants and civilians blurred, and the laws of war were utterly ignored. The battles over the bridges into Monrovia were so intense that the road was paved in blood and brass shells; lampposts, road signs, and nearby buildings were riddled with bullet holes. As John W. Blaney, the U.S. ambassador to Liberia, later recalled in an interview: "It was really like a 14th-century siege. The two rebel armies had surrounded Monrovia with the government's troops inside of Monrovia and the two rebel armies pressing hard outside."[27] Frustrated by AFL resistance, rebels started indiscriminately shelling the overcrowded inner city with mortars, killing more than 1,000 civilians.[28] Liberians described the situation as "World War III" and began piling their dead at the gates of the U.S. Embassy in a macabre plea for help.[29]

Monrovia was already a humanitarian disaster, as hundreds of thousands of internally displaced Liberians had fled the fighting in the hinterlands for the capital, which could not accommodate them all. With no electricity, water, sewage, police, food, or any other accoutrement of modern life, the city became a massive slum of tin shacks, garbage, human waste, disease, and lawlessness. Liberia was once the jewel of West Africa and a popular international vacation destination: Pam Am airlines had flown directly from New York City to Monrovia three times a week.[30] Now the country was apocalyptic.

International pressure mounted as the siege went on, stretching from days into weeks. U.S. President George W. Bush twice demanded on international television that Taylor "leave Liberia" and stationed 2,300 marines in three U.S. Navy ships off the country's shore.[31] Nigeria offered Taylor asylum if he left, shielding him from the machinations of international law.[32] The UN Security Council authorized a multinational peacekeeping force in Liberia, citing its deep concern over "the humanitarian situation, including the tragic loss of countless innocent lives . . . and its destabilising effect on the region."[33] Meanwhile, the Economic Community of West African States (ECOWAS), a regional international organization, hastily assembled a force to relieve the city.

With global pressure intensifying and rebels at the gates, Taylor finally yielded on August 11 and fled to Nigeria. He blamed Liberia's problems on foreign meddling and cast himself the martyr: "Because Jesus died, we are saved today. I want to be the sacrificial lamb. I am the whipping boy. It's easy to say 'It's because of Taylor'. After today, there will be no more Taylor to blame."[34] A few days later, the rebels lifted their siege, and 1,000 ECOWAS peacekeepers and 200 U.S. Marines entered the city to provide emergency humanitarian assistance and prevent a relapse of violence. "God bless you, Oga," women cried to convoys of Nigerians, using the Nigerian Yoruba word for "boss." "God bless you, Marine," they sang to other vehicles filled with American troops.[35] On August 18, the two rebel groups and what was left of Taylor's government signed a comprehensive peace agreement (CPA) at Accra, Ghana, ending Liberia's bloody civil war.[36]

However, a tragic legacy remained: After 150 years of troubled history, 14 years of civil war, and horrific abuses of power, Liberia was shattered. Its infrastructure was beyond destroyed, any semblance of civil governance had been long since abandoned, and much of its population was either displaced or dead. To this day, Liberia is plagued by intense hunger and poverty, no central running water or sewage, no telephone landlines, and no electrical grid. Small generators power most of the country.

The human cost was even greater. As a U.S. Agency for International Development (USAID) report describes, in a country of only three million:

> over 250,000 people, most of them civilian non-combatants, have lost their lives in the civil war. More than 1.3 million have been displaced, including hundreds of thousands who fled the country. Abductions, torture, rape and other human rights abuses have taken place on a massive scale. It is estimated that at least one in ten children may have been recruited into militias at one time or another. A similar percentage has been traumatised by seeing their families and friends murdered and raped.[37]

Almost everyone in Liberia was affected by the war. Post-conflict polls show that 96 percent of respondents had some direct experience of the conflict, and, of these, an astonishing 90 percent were at one point or another displaced from their homes.[38]

Liberia is a stark example of post-conflict state disintegration; as Africa expert Peter Pham observes, "Tragically, the recent history of Liberia has been a case study *par excellence* of a failed state."[39] Beginning with the first coup d'etat in 1980, national authority— if it even existed—rarely extended beyond Monrovia. Institutions were anemic, and those who possessed the means of violence served warlords such as Taylor rather than the state. Civilians were both the principal actors and targets of armed conflict, displacing nearly half the population and destabilizing the region.

By 2003, there were no functioning public utilities, and most Liberians still have no access to electricity, water, sanitation facilities, or health care. Basic infrastructure such as roads and bridges—which aid workers, entrepreneurs, peacekeepers, and Liberians themselves all need, especially in rural areas—are in dire need of repairs. A whole generation of Liberians received no formal education, and the country suffered a brain drain of those that did. Liberia has no functioning judicial system, leaving it with a culture of impunity: Most courts have been destroyed, and trial by ordeal is not unheard of outside the capital.

Historical Roots of the Conflict.

Like Ethiopia, Liberia never knew colonization. Freed African-American slaves and abolitionists founded it in 1822 with the help of the United States

26

as an outpost for other freed slaves returning from the Americas. The country's name is derived from the Latin word *liber,* meaning *free,* and its capital Monrovia was named in honor of U.S. President James Monroe, who held office at the country's founding and supported its creation. Liberia's red, white, and blue flag is modeled on the U.S. flag, and its currency is the Liberian dollar. The country was an eager and willing U.S. ally during World War II and the Cold War.

Growing from an outpost to a commonwealth, Liberia achieved statehood in 1847 with the ratification of a constitution drafted at Harvard University. However, problems loomed. Few of the freed slaves who found new beginnings in Liberia were from that region of Africa, and they proceeded to treat local tribes in ways comparable to their own treatment in the Americas. Soon a rift developed between descendants of the freed slaves, known as Americo-Liberians, and the 14 or so indigenous tribes. This evolved into a hierarchical caste system with four distinct classes. At the top were the elites: Americo-Liberian officials of mixed black and white ancestry with light skin (also known as mulattos). Second were darker-skinned Americo-Liberians, consisting mostly of laborers and small farmers. Third were the "recaptives" or "Congos," African captives on U.S.-bound slave ships who were rescued by the U.S. Navy and brought to Liberia. At the bottom of the hierarchy were the indigenous Liberians.[40] The first three classes—comprising less than 3 percent of the population—retained absolute political control, enjoyed a monopoly of social privilege, and benefitted substantially from the unequal distribution of power and wealth within the country. This tyranny of the elites went unabated until 1980, when a coup d'etat irrevocably altered the national landscape.

End of Americo-Liberian Rule.

The 1970s marked the beginning of the end for the elites' 125-year rule. In 1971, William Tubman, Liberia's president for 27 years, died while in office. His Open Door economic policy had proven a boon for Liberia, giving it the largest mercantile fleet and rubber industry in the world. The country also became the third-largest exporter of iron ore globally and received over $1 billion in foreign investment. Few, however, enjoyed the benefits, as the prospering Americo-Liberians tended not to share the wealth. This further widened the rift between the elites and the rest of the population, setting the conditions for revolt.

Tubman's vice president and successor, William Tolbert, attempted to ward off the crash course the country was on, but his own Americo-Liberian roots combined with the ensconced system of political and social elitism hindered his efforts. Adversaries almost immediately accused him of nepotism and cronyism. However, he also began to liberalize Liberia by introducing reforms to allow more indigenous Liberians in government and creating the first opposition party in the nation's history, the Progressive Alliance of Liberia, to run against the Americo-Liberians' old True Whig Party. Though re-elected in 1975, his government was criticized sharply for failing to address the deep economic disparities between the Americo-Liberians and the rest of the population. Social unrest began to swell as the majority felt change was occurring too slowly, while power-wielding Americo-Liberians felt it was too rapid.

Tensions came to a head in 1979. In April, Tolbert's administration proposed to raise the price of government-subsidized rice by 50 percent, claiming it would promote more local farming, slow the rate of urban migration, and reduce dependence on imported rice. Opposition leaders claimed the measure was meant only to benefit the Tolbert family, which controlled the rice monopoly in Liberia. Hundreds of people marched through Monrovia, protesting the sharp rise in the price of rice. Tolbert ordered troops to fire on the demonstrators, killing some 70 people. So-called rice riots soon spread throughout Liberia, and government attempts to quash them by arresting the opposition leaders failed. Tolbert's credibility was dealt a mortal blow, and the situation within Liberia continued to decay.

On April 12, 1980, AFL Master Sergeant Samuel Doe, an ethnic Krahn, led a coup d'etat, ending the 133-year monopoly of power that the Americo-Liberians' True Whig Party had enjoyed. The coup gained immediate popular acceptance, and Doe adopted the revolutionary slogan that "in the cause of the people, the struggle continues." Doe personally disemboweled Tolbert in his bed and then ordered the public execution of 13 top-ranking ministers and members of the Tolbert family. They were tied to poles on South Beach in Monrovia and shot to death. Many ranking government ministers who survived were tried, tortured, and paraded naked through downtown Monrovia. African countries, allies, and trading partners widely condemned the coup; a flight of capital and the elites soon ensued, including future president Ellen Johnson-Sirleaf.

The Reign of Samuel Doe: 1980–89.

Following the coup, Doe suspended the constitution and established the People's Redemption Council (PRC) with full powers, consisting of 17 enlisted men headed by Doe. The PRC imposed a price freeze on all commodities, including imported foods, and doubled the salaries of civil servants and military personnel. Doe lacked formal education, and, by many accounts, he was illiterate when he assumed the presidency. After only 1 year, he executed five PRC members, including his vice head of state and coup comrade Thomas Weh-Syen, claiming they had plotted against him. As he grew increasingly paranoid regarding threats to his leadership, he placed members of his own Krahn ethnic group in key positions. Soon the Krahn dominated the government, and as Africa expert Peter Pham notes, "The new regime turned increasingly brutal and proved even less popular than its predecessors."[41] Doe's inner circle became as disillusioned with the autocratic regime as was the general population. In November 1983, three prominent members of the PRC left Liberia: Thomas Quiwonkpa, who was the AFL's commanding general; Prince Yormie Johnson, Quiwonkpa's aide; and Charles Taylor, the head of the General Service Agency. All would eventually challenge Doe.

Doe further solidified control by holding elections in 1985, which were characterized by widespread fraud. Before the election, more than 50 of Doe's opponents were murdered, and most of the elected opposition candidates refused to take their seats. Liberia's political situation continued to erode with increased human rights abuses, corruption, and ethnic tensions. On November 12, 1985, Quiwonkpa staged a coup with an estimated 500 to 600 people from neighboring Sierra Leone; the AFL killed them all, and Quiwonkpa's body was dragged through Monrovia's streets. The Krahn-dominated AFL then retaliated against the ethnic groups in Quiwonkpa's native Nimba County, causing widespread loss of life within the Gio and Mano communities.

Despite Doe's poor human rights record and dubious democratic credentials, his regime enjoyed considerable U.S. financial and political support. Washington considered Monrovia an important strategic ally during the Cold War, and from 1981 to 1985, the United States gave Liberia $402 million in aid, more than Liberia had ever received before and more financial aid per capita than any other sub-Saharan country received during the 1980s.[42] Doe even met with President Ronald Reagan twice, and some have speculated that the U.S. endorsement of the 1985 election results—despite international and domestic observers' reports that it was compromised—may have led Doe to declare an unchallenged victory over his closest rival, Jackson F. Doe, whom many believed, and still maintain, was the true winner.[43]

The Reign of Charles Taylor: 1989–2003.

On Christmas Eve of 1989, Charles Taylor and approximately 100 fighters, some trained in Libya, invaded Liberia from neighboring Côte d'Ivoire. Named the National Patriotic Front of Liberia (NPFL), this rebel incursion initially enjoyed popular support within Nimba County, which had endured the majority of Samuel Doe's wrath after the 1985 attempted coup. Within 6 months, Taylor's forces reached the outskirts of Monrovia, but were stopped by AFL counterattacks.

A bloody civil war ensued, claiming hundreds of thousands of lives and displacing a million people in a country of only four million. The human toll of the 14-year war (1989–2003) is estimated at 270,000 dead, 320,000 long-term internally displaced people, and 75,000 refugees in neighboring countries. Almost everybody in Liberia was touched by the war: A recent poll shows that 96 percent of respondents had some direct experience of the conflict, and of these, a shocking 90 percent were at one point or another displaced from their homes.[44] The situation was so dire that ECOWAS, a regional international organization, intervened in 1990 under the premise of a cease-fire and peace deal, albeit without the NPFL. ECOWAS's peacekeeping force, the Economic Community of West African States Monitoring Group (ECOMOG), prevented the NPFL from entering Monrovia. However, the NPFL ravaged the Krahn and Mandingo areas of Liberia, with widespread atrocities reported. Although reports vary, Ellen Johnson-Sirleaf was apparently affiliated with Charles Taylor's movement.[45]

In July 1990, the NPFL splintered. Prince Johnson formed the Independent National Patriotic Front of Liberia (INPFL), which captured and killed Doe on September 9, 1990, torturing him on Monrovia's beach. AFL soldiers fled to Sierra Leone and founded the new insurgent United Liberation Movement of Liberia for Democracy (ULIMO). Soon after, an Interim Government of National Unity (IGNU), with Amos C. Sawyer as its president, was formed in Gambia with ECOWAS support. However, Taylor did not recognize the IGNU, and the fighting continued. By 1995, Liberia's civil war had grown to involve seven major factions, including the AFL, which acted as an armed political organ rather than a professional military. These seven factions joined to form the Liberian Council of State, in accordance with the 1995 Abuja Peace Accords. However, fighting still continued, and 1996 saw some of the war's deadliest battles.

Taylor finally agreed to a peace deal after more than a dozen peace accords and the exhaustion of his military power. A five-man transitional government was established, and warring factions were hastily disarmed and demobilized in advance of special elections, held on July 19, 1997. Taylor and his National Patriotic Party emerged victorious. Taylor himself won the election by a large majority, gaining 75 percent of the vote primarily because Liberians feared a return to war if Taylor lost. However, peace in Liberia did not last long. Taylor's government did nothing to improve the lives of Liberians: Unemployment and illiteracy stood above 75 percent, little investment was made in the country's infrastructure, reconciliation between factions was largely ignored, and rule of law was eclipsed by a patronage system that recognized Taylor as its supreme authority.

Taylor's actions not only exacerbated Liberia's intractable civil war; they helped foment civil war in Sierra Leone. Taylor backed the Revolutionary United Front (RUF), a Sierra Leonean rebel group, and reportedly directed RUF operations from Liberia. He is accused of selling them weapons in exchange for diamonds, which they typically extracted with slave labor and under threat of maiming or death; hence the term "blood diamonds." Owing to the UN embargo against arms sales to Liberia at the time, the weapons were purchased largely on the black market through arms smugglers such as Viktor Bout.[46] Taylor is also charged with aiding and abetting RUF atrocities against civilians and assisting in the recruitment of child soldiers.

Like Liberia's war, Sierra Leone's civil war was total. More than 200,000 of the country's 2.6 million people were killed. Approximately 800,000 were internally displaced, and another 700,000 sought refuge in neighboring countries. The fighting destroyed much of the country's infrastructure, including water and electricity. Sierra Leone's war also left it a ward of the international community under the protection of the UN Mission in Sierra Leone (UNAMSIL), which had a Chapter VII mandate. The UN declared UNAMSIL's mission complete in 2005, although the country remains precariously fragile.

Taylor's misrule at home led to the resumption of armed rebellion among his former adversaries. LURD was formed in 1999 and engaged in sporadic fighting with the AFL in northern Lofa County, which borders Guinea. It was headed by Sekou Conneh, a businessman married to the daughter of Guinean president Lansana Conté. By 2000, it was believed that LURD controlled nearly 80 percent of the countryside. Throughout the fighting, both the AFL and LURD were accused of widespread human rights violations as well as child soldier recruitment. In 2003, MODEL formed as an offshoot of LURD in Côte d'Ivoire and enjoyed support in the southeastern counties of Grand Gedeh, Sinoe, and Grand Kru. By the spring of 2003, LURD and MODEL had advanced to the outskirts of Monrovia, and intense fighting took place in and around the city. Thus began the siege of Monrovia.

With fighting escalating, Taylor agreed to participate in an ECOWAS-sponsored peace summit in Ghana between the government of Liberia, civil society, and the LURD and MODEL rebel groups. In the hope that Taylor's Ghanaian hosts would arrest him, the chief prosecutor of the UN-supported Special Court for Sierra Leone issued a press statement announcing the opening of a sealed March 7, 2003, indictment of Taylor for "bearing the greatest responsibility" for atrocities in Sierra Leone since November 1996.[47] Reportedly caught by surprise and unwilling to arrest Taylor, Ghana refused to detain him. Within hours, Taylor returned to Monrovia, where the fighting continued and intensified, creating a massive humanitarian disaster. Rebels indiscriminately fired mortars into downtown Monrovia, and the bodies of the innocent began to pile up.

U.S. Ambassador Blaney requested military assistance, and in response, the United States established Joint Task Force Liberia, comprised of three Navy ships and 2,300 troops of the 26th Marine Expeditionary Unit. This force positioned itself off the West African coast and sent a small number of Marines to protect the embassy, which had come under attack. At this point, the rebels were on the mainland trying to cross the bridges to inner-city Monrovia, which was heavily defended by Taylor's forces. During one of these firefights, Blaney walked onto the middle of a bridge and demanded both sides stop fighting. Amazingly, they did.[48]

Finally, on August 11, 2003, under intense international pressure, Taylor accepted an ECOWAS-brokered peace deal that offered him asylum in Nigeria. LURD, MODEL, and the Government of Liberia signed a comprehensive peace agreement in Accra, Ghana, on August 18, 2003, known as the Accra Accords. This paved the way for the deployment of what became a 3,600-strong ECOWAS peacekeeping mission in Liberia — ECOMIL — and also established a 2-year National Transitional Government of Liberia (NTGL), headed by Liberian businessman Gyude Bryant.

The UN Takes Charge.

The UN took over security duties in October 2003, subsuming ECOMIL into UNMIL, which had an authorized strength of 15,000 UN blue-helmet military personnel and 1,115 police officers, making it the world's largest UN peacekeeping mission at the time. UNMIL's mission as established by Security Council Resolution 1509 and led by Jacques Paul Klein was to monitor the ceasefire agreement, but it rapidly evolved into a rebuilding of the country. In terms of priorities, everything was urgent in Liberia: security, humanitarian relief, good governance, economic stabilization, democratization, and development. The NTGL nominally led Liberia as the UN prepared the country for elections in 2005, though many regarded the NTGL as a kleptocracy.[49]

The 2005 elections are considered the most free, fair, and peaceful elections in Liberia's history. The October 11, 2005, presidential and legislative elections, and the subsequent November 8, 2005, presidential run-off saw the victory of Ellen Johnson-Sirleaf, former World Bank official and human rights advocate, over George Weah, an international football star and former UN Children's Fund goodwill ambassador. Inaugurated in January 2006, President Johnson-Sirleaf, nicknamed the Iron Lady, is Africa's first democratically elected female president. Her government of technocrats draws from Liberia's many ethnic groups and also includes members of the Liberian diaspora — that is, those who had fled the country earlier. In March 2006, her reversal of an earlier position led to Charles Taylor being turned over to the Special Court for Sierra Leone.

The country has remained remarkably stable since the 2005 elections and may even serve as a model of post-conflict stability in a neo-medieval world. As Blaney and Klein observed in 2010:

> The country's future may not yet be secure, and much progress has yet to be made, but most of those present in the immediate aftermath of the war in 2003 would agree that today's Liberia is a comparative miracle.[50]

Johnson-Sirleaf has pursued an ambitious reconstruction agenda aimed at political stability and economic recovery, emphasizing job creation, education, attracting investment, and infrastructure repair, as well as restoration of public services, security sector reform, and a "government of inclusion." She has bolstered public trust by taking a strong stand against corruption, which is endemic in Liberia's political system. She has dismissed several government officials, including much of the Ministry of Finance, and supported experienced and technically competent senior officials. Her World Bank background has allowed her to forge strong relations with the international community and donor nations, which is crucial given Liberia's dependence on foreign aid.

Yet political conditions in Liberia are still perilous, as the roots of conflict have not been fully addressed, institutions are weak, development is still taking hold, the region of West Africa is unstable, and violence as a political solution is a precedent that cannot be ignored. To date, the UN ultimately guarantees Liberia's security, and grave concerns remain about the country's future once it departs. The country's prospects remain uncertain given the government's limited capacity, the dangerous geopolitical neighborhood it inhabits, and the many spoilers waiting in the wings. To survive as a state, a government needs a monopoly of force to uphold its rule of law and fend off armed threats to its existence.

SSR success is helped if it is required in formal peace treaties, giving it a clear mandate. In Liberia, the Accra Accords settled the civil war, and Part 4 specifically mandated SSR.[51] In sharing responsibilities for the process, UNMIL assumed the restructuring of civilian elements of the security sector, and the United States the transformation of the military sub-sector, owing to its historical ties to Liberia and especially its defense. The U.S. Navy guaranteed security during the 19th century; the United States oversaw the creation of the Liberian Frontier Force in 1908, used Liberia as a strategic logistical supply node for the North Africa campaign of World War II, and gave substantial military aid to Liberia during the Cold War. Also, as an internal Department of State (DoS) document explained, the "International community expects the US to take the lead in this endeavor. No other country will do so."[52] This monograph focuses on the U.S. program to transform the defense sector and does not address the UN's beleaguered efforts at reforming the Liberian National Police, which remains a critical problem today.

Outsourcing DDR and SSR.

The crucial task of rebuilding Liberia's military was outsourced to DynCorp International, which worked in parallel with the UN but not under it. DynCorp is a private military company (PMC), sometimes also called a private security company. PMCs are conflict entrepreneurs that kill or train others to kill, usually in foreign lands.[53] Contracting the wholesale reconstitution of a nation's armed forces to a private firm had not been attempted since the early 19th century and remains one of the most controversial facets of Liberia's recovery.

However, outsourcing DDR and SSR is a trend that will likely grow since these are not core capabilities of the DoD, and USAID is prohibited by law from defense development. This has left a gap that the private sector has increasingly filled in the Balkans, Iraq, Afghanistan, and elsewhere, and it will likely continue to do so. Privatizing functions like DDR and SSR affects program outcomes, so it is important to assess the potential impacts of this trend towards privatization. This makes Liberia an especially apt case study since it is the first time in a century or two that a sovereign nation hired a private company to raise another sovereign nation's armed forces.

The Liberia program is unique even from the programs in Iraq and Afghanistan in that it was entirely outsourced to the private sector. This was not entirely a bad thing, contrary to some of the dire warnings from skeptics that outsourcing *any* military function is undesirable. DynCorp's profit motive drove it to find innovative, efficient, and effective solutions to thorny security problems, and this accounts for some of Liberia's success today.

On the positive side, for example, the private sector brought a great deal of ingenuity to SSR. In 2004, there were no books, theory, best practices, military doctrine, compendia of lessons learned, or practitioners with significant experience on how to demobilize and rebuild an army. Scholarship was equally unhelpful, as it has always lagged behind practice in DDR and SSR. Owing to this, DynCorp's team invented new solutions to its specific DDR and SSR problems, resulting in a *sui generis* program that could serve as an imperfect yet necessary model for future DDR and SSR programs, and it did so in a post-conflict setting, one of the most difficult operating environments in the world.[54]

On the negative side, using private means to achieve public ends can sometimes pit profit motive against policy goals, and this created problems in the public-private partnership between the United States, DynCorp, and Liberia. Perhaps the most significant fact of DynCorp's work in Liberia is that the private sector can raise an army at all. This monograph does not fully explore these complex issues but does acknowledge them.

Decision to Outsource.

The U.S. Government did not originally intend to make history by outsourcing the building of Liberia's military; necessity drove the decision. The DoS was the client since it was responsible for managing U.S. commitments to Liberia as agreed to at Accra, including SSR for the AFL. To this end, the DoS organized a five-person SSR pre-assessment trip, made from January 21 to 29, 2004, with members from the DoS and DoD. The purpose was to better understand the general requirements for Liberia's military SSR in advance of a fuller assessment. After meeting with UN Chief Klein, U.S. Ambassador Blaney, Liberian Chairman Bryant (the title "President" was deemed inappropriate for a interim head of government), and leaders of the AFL, LURD, MODEL and others, the assessment team concluded that Liberia needed "a small, mobile defense force to provide border, coastal and internal security to support their mission" and estimated the size of the military should be from 3,000 to 6,500 personnel.

The pre-assessment team also observed United Kingdom (UK) efforts to rebuild the military of neighboring Sierra Leone and determined not to use the British model of SSR, concluding that "while IMATT [UK's International Military Assistance Training Team] was initially viewed as a success story in Sierra Leone, the UK now admit to many problems that they have yet to resolve." One of the primary challenges was dismissing the combatants thought to be human right violators while incorporating the rest into the new security forces regardless of their faction, experience, capability, or the country's security needs. Not surprisingly, this did not lead to SSR success.

This is the practice of *lustration*, and has been performed by the international community since at least World War II with mixed success. Lustration is the process of culling an existing security force, retaining desirable individuals, and dismissing the others. Examples include "denazification" (*Entnazifizierung*) of the German government after World War II, Greece in 1973 after a junta took control of the government and dismissed approximately 100,000 individuals from government and the military, and former Communist countries after the 1990s, passing lustration laws to drastically reduce the size of their governments, including the security sector. Individuals not cut or "lustrated" from the security sector are often merged into a single security force.

Lustration can be successful, as exemplified by denazification, or a failure, as demonstrated by "debathification" after the Iraq War. Sierra Leone was the latter. While lustration offers a convenient political solution for diplomats at the negotiation table, it creates significant problems on the ground, since former enemies are expected to function together as a fighting team in the new army. In Sierra Leone, it resulted in significant challenges in the quality control of troops and the sheer number of forces, which the government could not sustain. Also, which combatants should be kept as "good" versus those dismissed without vetting? No serious investigation was done of combatants in Sierra Leone, which permitted undesirable individuals in the ranks and defeated the purpose of the program. The UN favors lustration, which it used in the Balkans in the 1990s with mixed results. Not surprisingly, UNMIL later used lustration to rebuild the Liberian National Police force and achieved disappointing results, a stark contrast to the AFL.[55] Owing to this, lustration is not recommended for SSR.

Lastly, the team considered four options for who should conduct implementation: the U.S. military alone, the U.S. military with light contractor involvement, a contractor with light U.S. military involvement, or a contractor alone.[56] They would let a second SSR assessment trip combined with budget considerations decide the matter. The second trip took place on May 19-26, and included some 20 experts drawn from the DoS, the DoD's European Command (EUCOM, the unified command responsible for West Africa at the time), and three companies: DynCorp, Pacific Architects and Engineers (PA&E), and Military Professional Resources Inc. (MPRI).[57]

The purpose of this evaluation mission — during which one of the DoD civilian staff members was murdered — was to determine the operational requirements for SSR of the AFL and Ministry of Defence.[58] At the conclusion of the trip, the team proposed to the U.S. embassy a restructured AFL, which it called the New Armed Forces of Liberia (NAFL). The NAFL's mission would be "to defend and protect the people of Liberia and the sovereignty of the nation against external and internal threats and to effectively respond to humanitarian crisis." To achieve this, it would require an armed force of 4,020 personnel, consisting of one light infantry brigade (three infantry battalions, one engineer battalion, and one base support battalion), one maritime patrol battalion, one aerial reconnaissance company, one military police company, an AFL headquarters company, and a military band.[59]

However, other than the NAFL's mission and force structure, the U.S. Government team completely overlooked many thorny yet essential components of SSR, among them DDR for the legacy armed forces, a recruitment plan in a state with destroyed infrastructure and low literacy, a vetting plan for personnel in a country where war crimes were rampant and background checks nearly impossible, the restructuring of the Ministry of Defence, leadership selection, a national military strategy, fostering local ownership, and the domestic political ramifications of making a new military. There was no consideration for how Liberia's population would receive the re-creation of the military; many would not welcome it, given the AFL's troubled past, and the Accra Accords mandated that this be addressed. On June 10, DynCorp submitted its own 78-page assessment of SSR for the AFL to the DoS that addressed most of these concerns.

Following the assessment mission, the DoD quickly concluded it could not conduct the SSR program due to resource constraints and ongoing operations in Iraq and Afghanistan.[60] Consequently, the DoS was left with a Hobson's choice: Either outsource the entire DDR and SSR program to the private sector or have no program for the AFL. The DoS chose the former and made history without meaning to.

Purchasing a New Army.

On September 17, 2004, the DoS issued its Statement of Work (SOW) for rebuilding the Liberian military. It was only seven pages long. The objective and scope were deceptively simple: Assist the government of Liberia in recruiting, training, and equipping a new military beginning with 2,000 personnel. Consultations over the summer among the DoS, DoD, Dyn-Corp, and others concluded that the AFL should be a 2,000-person, all-volunteer force that could be scaled upward over time. It was acknowledged that 2,000 soldiers could not defend the entire country should a full-scale war erupt, but the size was constrained by the government's ability to regularly pay soldiers' salaries, as precedent suggested unpaid soldiers were a greater threat to Liberia's security than an invading army. Klein even suggested that Liberia abolish its military altogether, quipping that African armies "sit around playing cards and plotting coups."[61]

DynCorp and PA&E both bid on the project and after reviewing both proposals, the DoS decided to divide the duties between the two contractors, giving them different roles based on their expertise. DynCorp would perform the bulk of the SSR at both the operational and institutional levels. At the operational level, it would rebuild the AFL from the ground up, which entailed the designing, recruiting, vetting, training, equipping, and fielding of the new force. At the institutional level, it would also create a new Ministry of Defence and establish systems for personnel management, intelligence, force integration and planning, resource management, communications, information management, public affairs, procurement and acquisition, internal audit, and other ministerial functions. PA&E would build the logistical infrastructure, such as roads and military bases, necessary to support the AFL once the SSR was well under way, and also provide limited mentorship when the units were in place. Both firms were required to construct military bases and other facilities as needed, with DoS approval. Absent from the initial plan was the DDR of the legacy AFL, which was originally to be conducted by the Liberian government, but later fell to DynCorp owing to the Liberian government's lack of capacity.

In short, DynCorp was contracted to raise an army. The company was not contracted to perform SSR of the entire Liberian security sector, since UNMIL was transforming civilian actors, such as the police; and other entities were responsible for security sector governance, the legislature, and the national security strategy. DynCorp's work was limited to transforming the institutional and operational actors of the military sub-sector. The envisioned end was as an ethnically balanced, properly vetted, professionally trained, civilian led, and apolitical military capable of "defending the national sovereignty and in extremis, respond to natural disasters," as called for by the Accra Accords.[62]

DynCorp Goes to Liberia.

Three individuals spearheaded DynCorp's effort, including the author. Most of the first year was dedicated to designing the program, identifying implicit tasks, and engaging key stakeholders, with the assistance of the U.S. defense attaché to Liberia. Stakeholders included the legacy force, former rebels, the host government, the international community (those who were in Liberia), and civil society. Recent scholarship suggests that DynCorp did little or no outreach to Liberians to establish local ownership.[63] However, this is incorrect: DynCorp's chief interlocutor with Liberian civil society was appropriately the Liberian government, primarily through Minister of Defence Daniel Chea and later Brownie Samukai.

By July 2005, a vision for the new AFL and Ministry of Defence emerged along with guiding principles for its reconstitution. Because the program was designed by a company and not the U.S. military, DynCorp resisted the temptation to build a large army in the U.S. image, as has occurred in Afghanistan and Iraq with mixed results. Instead, the firm sought to craft—in partnership with the United States and Liberia—an armed force tailored to Liberia's unique regional needs.

Blueprint for the New Army.

It is impossible to truncate a multiyear, highly complex program—with more than a few surprises—into a monograph, and a brief timeline is included in an Annex to provide coherence. The original plan anticipated training beginning a few months after the National Training Program (NTP), but pre-program consultations and start-up operations took longer than expected. Working in a country as sacked and pillaged as Liberia is problematic; accomplishing even a straightforward task in a place without infrastructure, institutions, or social trust is grueling, like war itself. As Carl von Clausewitz reminds us, "everything in war is simple, but the simplest thing is difficult."[64]

Demobilizing the Legacy Force and Raising a New One.

Owing to the AFL's troubled legacy during the civil war and lack of records, lustration was viewed as sub-optimal since it was impossible to vet who was a "good guy." Instead, it was agreed upon that the old AFL should be completely demobilized and rebuilt to ensure systematic human rights vetting of new recruits and also assure the population that this really was a new AFL. Though this was a controversial decision at the time, it later spared the AFL from some of the challenges experienced by the Liberian National Police, where UNMIL practiced lustration resulting in a quasi-corrupt police force. But a corrupt security force that has lost public trust and legitimacy is a problem not easily undone. Indeed, the Liberian National Police remain a key obstacle to peace and security in Liberia today.

The governments of Liberia and the United States agreed that the new AFL would be open to all Liberians regardless of sex, tribe, or religion, and selection and promotion would be based on merit rather than cronyism or nepotism. Recruitment would maintain a 12th-grade functional literacy standard and work to achieve a balanced ethnic and gender mix within the ranks. All candidates would be vigorously vetted for past human rights abuses on an individual basis. Training would foster an apolitical professional ethos, especially in the leadership, that respected the rule of law, cultivated an ethos of public service, and accepted civilian control of the military.[65] Throughout the DDR and SSR process, DynCorp would manage a public sensitization program crafted mostly by local Liberians rather than international media consultants.

One key advantage that Liberia had over Iraq, Afghanistan, and elsewhere is security. First, UNMIL maintained an overwhelming force in the small country, with over 15,000 peacekeepers who acted as deterrent and hammer. This is in contrast with Iraq and Afghanistan, where coalition forces were spread too thin across an immense landscape and could not control it, a clear violation of T. E. Lawrence's "Algebraic Principle."[66] Also, Liberians genuinely had war fatigue, in the author's opinion. Few desired to return to a state of unbridled horror as demonstrated by Doe and Taylor and were content to let the UN take over. Consequently, there was no significant insurgent movement to challenge the peacekeeping force. This might grimly suggest that post-conflict recovery best begins after war has run its course.

Human Security as Unifying Concept.

After DynCorp's initial assessment of Liberia's defense sector in May 2004, the company had judged that the greatest risks to Liberian security were not strong neighboring states with powerful armies threatening invasions, but rather violent street crime, criminal militias, disease and poverty, armed insurrection, food insecurity, lack of access to justice and political representation, terrorism, and a dearth of the basic necessities of life—all internally driven conditions arising from failures of development and good governance. Armed nonstate actors could exploit these public grievances for active or passive support. Examples of active support include providing logistical help or sanctuary to militias; passive support entails not cooperating with authorities regarding the whereabouts and activities of anti-government groups. Doe, Taylor, LURD, and MODEL all depended on both types of support in their rise to power.

Based on this threat assessment, DynCorp believed Liberians (and the DoS) would judge the AFL's success by its ability to secure development rather than repel invaders.[67] Historically, when the U.S. military builds foreign armies, it attempts to create a force that mirrors its own: conventional units strong enough to physically defend the borders against armed aggressors and also project force abroad when needed. Strong armies are effective at waging regular warfare—interstate, military-on-military engagements, also known as "conventional war" like World War II—but less so when dealing with irregular threats and nonstate actors that gain support and sanctuary by exploiting popular grievances that stem from failures of development and good governance, as was the case in Liberia.[68]

Accordingly, DynCorp abandoned the regular approach to SSR and adopted a novel paradigm when designing the Liberian defense architecture and strategy—"human security"—marking one of the earliest attempts to operationalize this idea. The conventional model of "national security" privileges its namesake: states. Steeped in the Westphalian tradition, the primary geopolitical actor is the state, which survives by checking other states' power though the Machiavellian calculus of national interests and balance-of-power politics, with military might as the ultimate arbiter. Westphalian warfare is the war of Clausewitz, World Wars I and II, nominally obeys the "laws of war," and constitutes "regular" warfare. Such a paradigm holds that if one secures the state, then security will cascade from the state down to the regime, community, and finally the individual.

The human security paradigm is the exact opposite. It best suits the non-Westphalian world of Africa and elsewhere, where states did not develop organically as they did in Europe and North America but rather were invented by cartographers in London, Paris, Berlin, and other colonizing powers of the past. Not surprisingly, this is a world were "irregular" warfare is more regular than "regular" warfare, as nonstate actors fight without regard for the laws of war that regulate interstate conflict.

Human security was a concept first articulated in the 1994 UN Development Program's (UNDP) *Human Development Report* and views security and development as inextricably linked and mutually reinforcing. The report argues that national security matters less when "several states are beginning to disintegrate," and the primary threats to global insecurity stem from failures of development — drugs, AIDS, terrorism, pollution, nuclear proliferation, and corruption — rather than strong rival states, as the Westphalian national security model presumes. These new threats "respect no national border," and "the search for human security lies in development, not in arms."[69] Consequently, the human security approach holds that if the individual is secured, then security will emanate to the community, regime, and finally the state. The national and human security paradigms are opposite understandings on how human communities are best protected (see Figure 2).

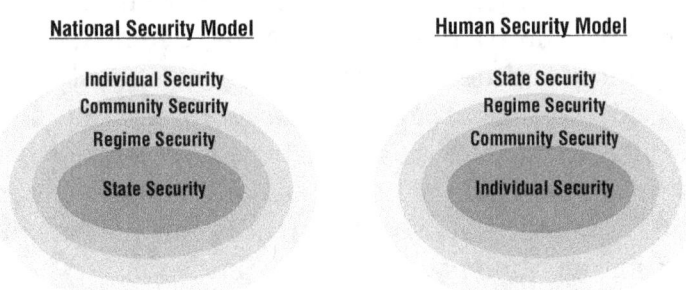

National Security Model

Individual Security
Community Security
Regime Security
State Security

Human Security Model

State Security
Regime Security
Community Security
Individual Security

Figure 2. National Versus Human Security Paradigms.

Owing to the threat assessment, DynCorp believed the human security paradigm would be a more appropriate model for the design and deployment of the AFL than the conventional national security one. Specifically, this meant de-emphasizing traditional missions, like defending national borders with a massive military, and securing development as the unifying concept behind the new AFL. The DoS and the Liberian government agreed with this idea, and in 2006, the author assisted the Minister of Defence in drafting the *National Defence Strategy* (NDS) white paper based on human security, making Liberia one of the first countries to try to operationalize human security in its military. The first sentence of the draft reads: "There can be no development without adequate security, nor can security be maintained without development and the benefits it promises for our population."[70]

From there, the strategy explained the relationship between security and development in the context of Liberia, identified Liberia's core security interests in light of development, and outlined the principles that informed AFL SSR. Beyond this, the strategy remained vague and not fully operational, and ultimately was transmuted into a more conventional defense strategy by external parties. However, human security ideas infused the SSR program, such as integrating civics and literacy classes as the major component of basic training, establishing an ethnically balanced force that is inclusive of women, creating an ombudsman position at Ministry of Defence, and holding peace-keeping and humanitarian assistance as central military missions.

The force structure of the new AFL and Ministry of Defence was designed to be strong enough to repel limited cross-border attacks but not so strong as to threaten Liberia's neighbors. This entailed a small, basic, well-trained motorized light infantry regiment without heavy or expensive weaponry, such as artillery, armor, or fighter planes. The plan also proscribed the creation of special forces and other secretive, elite units that could easily become politicized killing machines, as the former Anti Terrorist Unit, the Special Anti Terrorist Unit, the Black Berets, the Special Security Service, and the Special Operations Division became during the civil war. Political leaders had abused these units in the past, using them as sectarian hit squads. The U.S. and Liberian governments did not wish to see a relapse of this tragic pattern.

On July 17, 2005, DynCorp proposed an initial force structure and table of organization and equipment (TO&E) — the blueprint for the new AFL — to the DoS. A TO&E is a master inventory of all personnel and equipment within the military, delineating for each unit the exact number, rank, title, and military occupational specialty of every individual and the name and quantity of each piece of equipment. Several models of the AFL and MOD were considered, including ones with agricultural battalions so the AFL could source its own food (rejected because it could lead to corruption within the ranks) and a robust engineer battalion to help rebuild the country and strengthen bonds with the local populace (rejected because it was too expensive).

The initial blueprint presented to and approved by the DoS in 2005 called for an AFL of just under 2,000 soldiers, comprising a brigade headquarters company, two light infantry battalions, an engineer company, a military police company, a training company, a military band, and three military personnel (in the Ministry of Defence). The Ministry of Defence was a lean 100 people, and all but three were civilians. This blueprint has changed over time, but the original concept for the AFL remains.

Program Stages.

The SSR program was originally envisaged as proceeding in several steps. In reality, the program's progression was ambiguous and fluid due to intervening challenges, though in retrospect, it had three relatively distinct phases. During this time, security was provided by UNMIL's large peacekeeping force.

Phase I began when the DoS decided to outsource the SSR program to the private sector and involved a small team of contractors to design the program and meet with stakeholders. Phase II commenced on May 15, 2005, when Chairman Bryant signed Executive Order Number Five authorizing the full demobilization of the legacy AFL on June 30, 2005.[71] After this, the DoS issued DynCorp an NTP for the program in full, and the company began to recruit and train staff (both local and international), acquire compounds and equipment for operations, construct a customized DDR site outside of Monrovia, demobilize 13,770 members of the legacy AFL, plan the public sensitization campaign regarding the AFL reconstitution, and formulate a systematic recruiting and vetting plan.

Phase III began in January 2006 with the completion of the old force's demobilization and the start of recruiting the new force. This phase involved a national public sensitization and recruiting campaign, rigorous vetting, creation of a basic training or initial entry training (IET) course, and Ministry of Defence training. It also required equipping the new force, legally purchasing and shipping arms to Liberia from Eastern Europe, and building the necessary bases. Determining entry standards for recruitment in the hopes of instilling a professional, apolitical ethos that placed service to the country above tribe or individual was problematic. Many Liberians were not sufficiently literate. Attracting women to the AFL was difficult because men historically filled the ranks. Vetting candidates and selecting leadership was complicated by a lack of public records. All AFL policies had to be created, while simultaneously transforming the Ministry of Defence, hiring and training all its civilian personnel, and synchronizing its development with that of the larger government.

Phase IV entailed fielding the new force and program termination. PA&E was responsible for constructing all nontraining military facilities, settling individual soldiers into units once they left training, and providing unit mentors. In 2009, Liberia's two infantry battalions underwent a certification exercise modeled on the U.S. Army Readiness Training Evaluation Program (ARTEP). The contract ended in 2010, and a team of 60 U.S. Marines begin a 5-year mentorship program with the AFL called Operation ONWARD LIBERTY.[72] Today, the AFL continues its development, transformed from an instrument of terror into one of stability. The International Crisis Group (ICG), a watchdog nongovernmental organization (NGO), assessed that "the SSR program, in particular army reform, is a provisional success."[73]

As with any complex, high stakes, post-conflict program, there were many problems. Problems internal to the program are examined in the text to follow. There were also many external surprises that slowed the program, costing the United States money, the company time, and Liberia its defense. Construction was expensive and delayed, as many materials had to be imported, theft was rampant, and concrete did not dry well in the monsoon-like rainy season from April to September. Building the new training base—and all training—was suspended for 8 months as Liberia, the United States, and UNMIL debated the base's location. Finally, in July 2006, the former Voice of America transmitter site was selected at Careysburg and rechristened the Sandee S. Ware Military Barracks.[74] DynCorp started construction once the occupying UNMIL units moved off site, which took much longer than expected. Another major surprise was the NTGL's inability to safely demobilize the legacy AFL, as was originally planned in 2004. By the spring of 2005, it became evident to the DoS that the NTGL could not demobilize its own troops, so it asked DynCorp to do so.

Chief among the challenges of Phase II was demobilizing Liberia's standing army peacefully, while continuing to maintain security. This included determining who was eligible for demobilization benefits, finding donor money to pay for those benefits, trying to prevent fraud, and anticipating unwelcome public response amid fears that disgruntled demobilized soldiers would incite political violence. Building the site on the outskirts of Monrovia involved its own challenges: finding competent construction companies, theft of materials, and significant delays caused by the rainy season. Other unexpected obstacles arose.

Razing an Army: Que Sera Sera.

Demobilizing a standing African army is tricky. Few — if any — modern African armies have faded away peacefully, as demonstrated by Liberia's neighbor, Côte d'Ivoire. Attempts by the U.S. military to retire forces in Iraq and Afghanistan have often led to greater insurgency and violence. In Liberia, there was no such resistance. By the time the UN intervened, there seemed to be genuine war fatigue in the country, but the lack of violence is also due to the manner in which DynCorp demobilized the old AFL.

On May 18, 2005, Chairman Bryant publicly proclaimed Executive Order Number Five at a national press conference in the presidential palace; as his entourage departed, the AFL band played "Que Sera Sera." The order, which had the force of law, declared the entire AFL officially decommissioned on June 30, 2005. Afterwards, Minster of Defence Chea told reporters that the demobilization exercise would take place in the months ahead and would be done by DynCorp, expressing confidence in the company. At the time, there was a real fear that members of the AFL would dig up cached weapons and challenge the authority of the state or demand greater remuneration in exchange for cooperation. Luckily, no such violence occurred, but it was a constant worry: For example, in April 2006, 400 to 500 ex-soldiers threatened there would be "no Christmas" if they did not receive salary arrears for their service.[75]

Immediately following the chairman's announcement, DynCorp got to work. First, it coordinated with UNMIL to provide security during the demobilization in case violence erupted — though the company's small armed presence would have been insufficient to put down a large armed riot. Next, the company subcontracted a local architecture and engineering firm to custom build a demobilization site on the outskirts of Monrovia, which was close enough to the city to be accessible for the majority of the population yet far enough to contain a violent outbreak before it spread to the capital. DynCorp also began refurbishing the Barclay Training Centre, a former AFL base in downtown Monrovia, and would later build the larger training base in Careysburg.

DynCorp's ability to rapidly demobilize the legacy AFL was aided by circumstance since it did not have to disarm combatants or determine who was eligible for benefits, both dangerous and time-consuming issues. UNMIL's DDRR (the extra "R" stands for Rehabilitation) program had already disarmed but not demobilized ex-AFL soldiers, who were confined to their barracks. However, as with LURD and MODEL, it was widely believed that the AFL's best weapons remained hidden rather than surrendered to UNMIL as a hedge against future hostilities. UNMIL collected few heavy or crew-served weapons despite their prevalence during the civil war, casting a shadow of anxiety over the entire process.

The NTGL rather than DynCorp decided who was eligible for demobilization benefits. Based on available funding, DynCorp derived a points system to distribute payment to ex-AFL fighters based on time in service and rank, which the NTGL approved and adopted. The minimum payment to help soldiers reintegrate into civil society was $540 (about a year's salary) and the maximum was over $2,000, substantially more than the flat $300 UNMIL offered nongovernment combatants in its DDRR program. Like so many other DDR programs, little was done to ensure long-term reintegration. Once individuals received their payments, they usually were offered transport to their home town and then forgotten. There was little, if any, serious job training, counseling, or similar assistance to prevent them from relying on violence to make a living. Also, there was no separate assistance for dependents of former soldiers, aside from the 270 widows who received compensation only after vociferous and persistent political protests to the Liberian government. But to be fair to DynCorp, it was not contracted to provide long-term assistance for former soldiers, only to demobilize them safely.

Not surprisingly, many Liberians fraudulently claimed they were in the AFL and demanded payment; determining who was actually in the AFL was difficult. First, nearly all the AFL personnel records were destroyed in the war. Second, many combatants took a *nom de guerre* during the war: memorable warlords include General Cobra, General Mosquito, General Mosquito Spray, General Peanut-Butter (currently a senator), and General Butt Naked (currently a preacher), whose warriors fought *au naturel*. Lastly, there was widespread fraud and abuse during UNMIL's DDRR process, as later vetting investigations revealed, giving precedent to cheating the system.[76]

In reference to the previous discussion, a large re-documentation exercise was launched to ascertain who was truly in the AFL, which the NTGL led and DynCorp operationalized. The executive order established a joint Demobilization Advisory Monitoring Committee (DAMC) to oversee the process, which did not include the firm.[77] Initially, well over 15,000 individuals claimed to be former AFL, but this list was painstakingly whittled down. UNMIL identified several hundred double dippers—Liberians who had already received benefits from UNMIL's DDRR program posing as members of LURD or MODEL. These individuals were disqualified from receiving additional pay-outs. The AFL leadership also reconstructed former unit rosters drawn from fragments of surviving records and considered every claim individually, using eight criteria to validate a veteran's identity.[78] Suspicious candidates were quizzed on life in the AFL: which unit they were in, where they served, who were their commanding officers and first sergeants. By the end of July, the NTGL produced a list of 13,500 ex-AFL members eligible for benefits and added 270 widows later for a total of 13,770.

Concurrent to these events, DynCorp and a senior member of the Ministry of Defence co-led a planning team of eight AFL officers that reported directly to the defense minister.[79] The team issued a military operations order that provided a demobilization schedule for all 27 units, a three-stage plan of action for the process (identity verification, registration, and payment), and logistical requirements and taskings.[80] Though successful, this hybrid team, led by a Liberian and a contractor, raised questions over where the NTGL's influence ended and DynCorp's began. The company had to manage significant portions of the process owing to the NTGL's lack of capacity, which raised concerns over who truly controlled the process.

The NTGL and DynCorp imbued the process with dignity, which encouraged participation. After years of war rife with human rights violations, it was tempting to treat the AFL as criminals rather than soldiers. This would have been a mistake. First, not everyone in the AFL committed war crimes. Second, criminalizing the process only would have alienated former AFL and deterred their cooperation, which was essential to the program. DynCorp consciously framed the demobilization as a retirement, modeled on the U.S. Army's own protocol, rather than a DDR pay-out to "thugs." Every day, a unit mustered at the demobilization site to be honored with a formal ceremony replete with protocol, the AFL band, and a congratulatory speech by the Minister of Defence or similar dignitary. Individuals then began the demobilization process, which verified and logged their identity, took an identification picture, and electronically fingerprinted them (see Figure 3). Following this, ex-soldiers received a voucher for payment at a Monrovian bank as well as a demobilization certificate and a card indicating that they were either "demobilized" or "honorably retired" (for those whose service began before Taylor's takeover). These documents were intended to provide a measure of closure and status to ex-combatants, but also, as official government papers, they represented the state's reconstitution after a long absence.

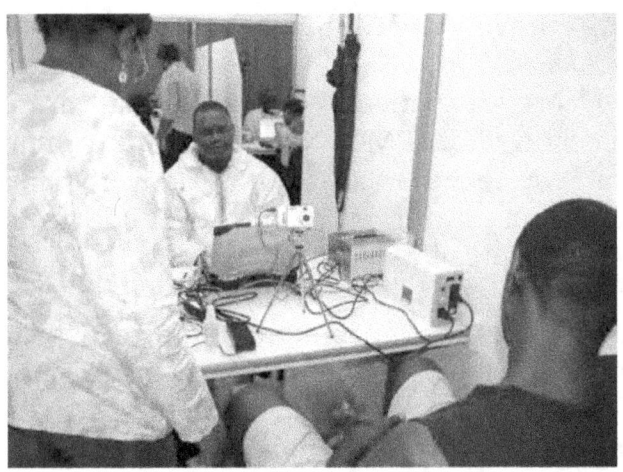

**Figure 3. One of 15 Demobilization Stations
with Biometric Capture at
DynCorp's Custom-Built Demobilization Site.**

Cynics might argue this was merely political the-
ater, yet, to date, it has been successful: The legacy
military remains peacefully demobilized. Moreover, it
was done safely and efficiently. By treating ex-combatants as soldiers rather than criminals, in 4 months
and at a cost of only $15 million, one of the more noto-
rious armies in Africa was completely and safely demobilized, a rare event in African history.[81] DynCorp's
ability to demobilize an army exemplifies what the
private military industry can do and perhaps where it
is heading within the new neo-medieval order. In the
new market for force, like the old, dismantling armed
challengers is the first step to gaining a monopoly of
force, whether it is for a client like Liberia—or the
PMC's own interests.

Raising an Army in Five Steps.

DynCorp's experience raising a small army for Liberia shows how PMCs today can build a military. Unlike PMC experiences in Iraq and Afghanistan, DynCorp raised an army with no support from the DoD and minimal assistance from the U.S. Government, other than payment. This is significant because it demonstrates the capability of the private sector to generate security forces today. Nor is DynCorp unique in its capacity.

Raising an army is obviously complex, and a full analysis of how it is done is beyond the scope of this monograph. Instead, an overview of five key elements of army building, all managed by DynCorp in Liberia, are discussed: (1) public sensitization, (2) recruiting, (3) vetting, (4) training and equipping, and (5) formulating strategy and institutional support.

Step 1: Alert the Public.

The first step in creating a new force—unless it is clandestine—is to alert the public. In Liberia, this was challenging, owing to the grim legacy of the former AFL in the war. Many Liberians, and even UNMIL's Jacques Klein, did not welcome this development and thought the country ought to adopt the Costa Rican model of a robust national police force in lieu of a military. However, ultimately it was decided during the Accra Peace Accords that Liberia needed a military because of the dangerous geopolitics of West Africa. To help prepare the populace for this, DynCorp began planning a public sensitization program in early 2005.

Major obstacles of any foreign-led messaging campaign are cultural and language barriers, and Liberia has 16 different tribes with their own customs and languages. The widely-spoken Liberian English is not easily recognizable to international English speakers, as it is a creole of Kru pidgin English and 19th-century African American vernacular English.[82] Moreover, the 14-year dearth of education due to the civil war and resultant 75 percent illiteracy rate limited much communication to oral or pictorial transmission. Due to these challenges, DynCorp sought to partner with a local communications firm and employed Liberians to craft effective messages that would resonate with indigenous audiences. DynCorp's role was confined mostly to logistical support and coordination with international community representatives in Liberia.

The communications strategy was a combined sensitization and recruitment campaign targeting opinion leaders, civil society, and the AFL recruitment pool. It consisted of several parallel efforts. The first was a series of workshops for senior AFL officers, cabinet members, soldiers to be demobilized, the media, and civil society groups. The second was a broader outreach campaign to the public as a whole and involved members of the government and the AFL SSR program who gave interviews to the media, debated on radio talk shows, staged rallies featuring other senior members of the government (see Figure 4), produced radio dramas featuring the AFL, placed ads in newspapers, displayed large AFL billboards and murals (see Figure 5), and recruited tours in Liberia's hinterlands (see Figure 6). DynCorp even commissioned AFL comic books titled *Jackie's Adventure* and *Liberia's New Armed Forces* for free distribution (see Figure 7). The company also set up two information booths in downtown Monrovia staffed by Liberians to answer any questions passers-by had regarding the AFL SSR process or how to enlist.

Figure 4. The Liberian Minister of National Defence Brownie Samukai at a Rally for the AFL, Coordinated by DynCorp in Monrovia, 2006.

Figure 5. The Author Standing in Front of an AFL Billboard Alerting the Public to the New Armed Forces of Liberia.

Figure 6. Part of a DynCorp Recruiting Convoy into the Hinterlands of Liberia.

Figure 7. DynCorp commissioned comic books to reach low-literacy audiences aimed at sharing information regarding the new AFL as well as encourage recruitment, especially among women in this case.

Despite DynCorp's efforts to localize the campaign by hiring locals to help design it, many Liberians found it bumbling and even insulting. The use of well-dressed and healthy-looking children on some of the AFL recruiting posters was not well received by a population traumatized by child soldiers. Many asked whether the children on the posters were American, given their health. This demonstrated a lack of cultural sensitivity on the part of the campaign designers, partly because the messages were not thoroughly tested on Liberian focus groups before they went public. Similarly, the comic books received mixed reactions; they were an effective tool for illiterate audiences but repelled some educated Liberians, who found them infantilizing.

Worse, DynCorp's attempt to combine sensitization and recruiting into a single campaign to conserve resources and time muddled messages and hampered the efficacy of both. In many ways, these two information efforts are incompatible. The objective of the sensitization program is to alert the public to the new military's formation in the most transparent and neutral manner possible, whereas the purpose of recruitment is advocacy by framing information in a highly positive way to encourage enlistment. DynCorp chose to prioritize recruitment over sensitization, which should not be a surprise. After all, it was hired to raise an army, not facilitate a civil society discourse on the role of the new AFL: Too much indigenous criticism of what it was doing could have resulted in the DoS cancelling its contract. But this lack of transparency and civil society engagement is an important component of SSR, as it inculcates ownership and acceptance of the new AFL.

Step 2: Recruiting.

Recruitment for the new AFL began on January 18, 2006, at the Barclay Training Center (BTC) in downtown Monrovia and attracted a great deal of attention, with a line wrapping nearly around the block (see Figure 8). Large groups of applicants even camped in front of the BTC for several nights before the opening day, and individuals travelled from outlying counties to stand for the chance to apply. In the first 2 months alone, DynCorp processed 4,000 applications.

Figure 8. The First Day of Recruiting Attracted a Long Line of Volunteers.

Most of the recruiting took place at the BTC because a third of the population was encamped at Monrovia, making it fertile enlisting ground, and BTC also had the infrastructure to support the operation. Neither the Liberian government nor the DoS desired an all-Monrovian military, but access to Liberia's interior was very limited. The few roads and bridges that existed were in poor shape, and some were impassable during the rainy season. To overcome this, DynCorp conducted large recruiting expeditions with the precision and robustness of a military operation. Each so-called forward recruiting convoy consisted of some dozen or so trucks, 50 staff, and all necessary equipment, including spare vehicles. They would deploy days and even weeks at a time to all 14 counties in Liberia and could process about 120 applicants a day. Like a military column, these forward recruitment operations consisted of several parts. Ahead of the main convoy, a reconnaissance team scouted the routes, conducted liaisons with relevant UN and Liberian authorities, and identified recruitment sites. Next, a public affairs team made radio announcements and distributed posters and comic books. Then the forward recruiting team's main body arrived, making announcements over truck-mounted speakers while driving through population centers. In the first 6 months of 2006, DynCorp launched 28 recruiting expeditions.

The final phase of the recruitment campaign was, of course, the recruitment itself. DynCorp devised a four-stage recruitment process—enlistment, a literacy aptitude test, a physical fitness test, and a medical exam—to select the best candidates from the recruitment pool. The stages were sequential: Applicants had to pass minimum acceptability standards before advancing to the next stage. To save money, DynCorp conducted less expensive tests first when the applicant pool was large, and more costly tests last when the applicant pool was smallest. This process is illustrated in Figure 9.

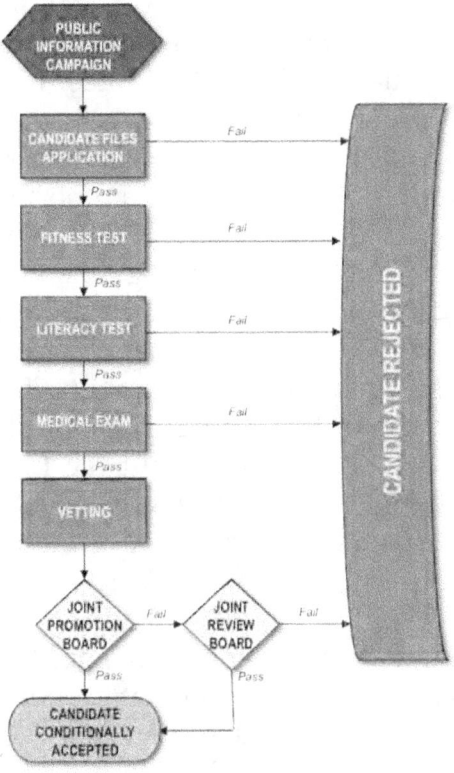

Figure 9. Recruiting Process.

The first stage of recruitment was enlistment. Applicants had to be Liberian citizens between the ages of 18 and 35, functionally literate at a 12th grade level for enlisted soldiers and at a college graduate level for officers, physically fit and healthy, without a criminal record, and free of allegations of human rights violations, crimes against humanity, or war crimes. Applicants showed up at a recruitment station and were searched for weapons, then asked to read a few simple sentences to ensure basic literacy (a fuller literacy exam ensued later); 11.5 percent failed this and were escorted off the premises. Applicants who could read were briefed on the AFL and the recruitment process. If individuals wished to volunteer to serve, they filed an enlistment application, received an AFL recruitment identity card with their picture and unique tracking number, and were given a report date for the second stage.

The second stage was assessing functional literacy. Soldiers had to be able to read and write orders, reports, maps, and other communications, a significant recruiting challenge in a country with 75 percent illiteracy. Because of this, DynCorp suggested a minimum 6th-grade reading level, but the Liberian government insisted on a 12th-grade level. Instead of relying on disparate and potentially fraudulent diplomas, DynCorp asked the West African Examinations Council (WAEC), a regional organization, to create an aptitude test that the company could administer. WAEC is a not-for-profit examination board that has administered standardized tests for 6th and 12th graders throughout the region since 1952. WAEC created a 90-minute aptitude test consisting of 30 multiple-choice questions and one essay to test for educational equivalency. If the applicant passed the aptitude test, he or she was invited to return the next day for a physical fitness test and medical exam; if the applicant failed the aptitude test, (s)he was given one more chance to retake the test in 28 days' time. Female candidates tended to score higher than males, and unlike in a developed country, younger Liberians on average did worse than older applicants, owing to the lack of schooling during the 14-year civil war. Fifty-eight percent of applicants passed this stage.

The third stage assessed physical aptitude. Obviously, strong physical prowess is a prerequisite for soldiering, and DynCorp modified the U.S. Army's physical fitness test to assess it, because the test required no special equipment or venue. To pass the test, applicants had to complete a minimum number of push-ups and sit-ups in a 2-minute time frame and run 1.5 miles in less than a specified time, depending on age and gender. Only 7.6 percent of applicants failed the fitness test, and these could retest in 28 days. Of those who failed, 58 percent failed to do the minimum required push-ups, 36 percent failed to complete the minimum required sit-ups, and 6 percent did not finish the 1.5 mile run in the maximum time allotted. Not surprisingly, applicants older than 34 had a higher failure rate than younger candidates, although the rate never exceeded 20 percent for any age group. Forty-eight percent of original applicants passed through this stage.

Next, applicants underwent a basic medical examination consisting of a general check-up, a drug screen, a tuberculosis test, and an HIV-AIDS test. Unlike the other tests, applicants who failed this exam were denied entry into the AFL unless it was for a temporary illness or the need of corrective lenses, in which case the applicant could return for a reexamination. Surprisingly, only 11.9 percent failed the medical examination during the first 6 months, mostly due to illegal drug use. Liberia has a relatively high HIV-AIDS rate, but the recruitment campaign's active dissemination of minimum entry standards may have deterred those afflicted from volunteering.

In sum, the purpose of the recruiting process is to select the best qualified individuals for service. However, this is not limited to technical skills alone. A key aspect of SSR is ensuring that no person of improper character is accepted into the new force, and this requires careful vetting of applicants.

Step 3. Vetting.

Vetting is perhaps the most important, yet inexplicably overlooked, element of raising security forces. Recruiting soldiers or policemen without proper background checks would be unthinkable in the United States, yet it has happened routinely in Iraq, Afghanistan, and other conflict affected states, which arguably need professional security services the most. The lack of rigorous vetting allows terrorists and criminals to easily infiltrate security forces and commit crimes in uniform, discrediting, and corrupting the force, while terrorizing the populace. On February 22, 2006, insurgents posing as Iraqi police destroyed the Golden Mosque in Samarra, one of Iraq's holiest Shiite shrines, re-igniting long-standing violence between Sunni and Shia in Iraq. This problem became so widespread in the Iraqi national police that in 2007, the U.S. Congress appointed a high-level independent commission headed by retired general James Jones, the former NATO commander, to assess the situation. The commission's recommendation was grim: "We should start over," meaning the SSR of the Iraqi police. But as an earlier inspector general report on the same topic observed, a corrupt security force that has lost public trust and legitimacy is "a problem not easily undone."[83]

One reason vetting is ignored is because it is hard. How does one conduct background checks in a failed state where there are few, if any, records kept? Background investigations normally rely on a plethora of records: criminal, commercial, financial, educational, and public. In a post-conflict failed state, such records may not have survived the war, if they existed in the first place; they also may be incomplete or not credible. In Liberia, what records remained were scant, incomplete, and generally untrustworthy, since forgery and identity theft were common. The AFL's personnel or G-1 Section of the Ministry of Defence had lost most of its filing systems, including the 201 files of its Military Personnel Record Jacket, which had documents on each soldier. Compounding the issue was the sheer number of problematic candidates, where many people were perpetrators or victims (or both) of violence during the war. The lack of tools plus the large volume of troubled backgrounds made human rights vetting a daunting challenge.

Vetting was also dangerous. Many did not welcome unearthing the bloody past, especially violent individuals under investigation with something to hide. If the vetting process failed to safeguard the identities of victims and witnesses who helped identify perpetrators, then those victims or SSR staff could be intimidated, coerced, and even killed in reprisal. If the vetting process accidentally admitted a war criminal, it would discredit all vetted individuals and perhaps even provoke a violent backlash. Wrongful denunciations made against innocent individuals could generate antagonism in the community and discredit the SSR program as a whole, deterring people from enlisting in the new army and defeating the purpose of the SSR effort.

DynCorp thus created an entirely novel approach to human rights vetting in post-conflict countries which the ICG says is "a notable success—the best, several experts said, they had witnessed anywhere in the world."[84] It combined investigative techniques, international best practices, and human rights norms to judge a candidate's character and capacity for a position of trust and to identify potential risks for security reasons.

We would never put a policeman or a soldier on the streets of a U.S. city without a thorough background check, yet such precautions are frequently neglected in conflict zones. To date, no public military or government has developed a systematic method for vetting in fragile states, which accounts for difficulties in Iraq and Afghanistan, for instance, where insurgents easily infiltrate the security forces and commit crimes in uniform. To avoid spoilers subverting the AFL, DynCorp invested in developing a new vetting model and did so more efficiently than the U.S. military, taking just a few months with a handful of experts. The U.S. military did not rigorously vet individuals who wished to serve in the Afghan, Iraqi, or similar security forces, despite its centrality to effective SSR.

The process utilized three methods: background checks, records checks, and public vetting. The vetting staff was compartmentalized from the recruiting office to avoid conflict of interest issues or selection bias. Once an applicant's file was passed to the vetting office, it was assigned to a background investigator, who worked closely with Liberian colleagues. The purpose was to establish the overall truthfulness of the applicants' claims about themselves and uncover evidence of past wrongdoing that would disqualify them from serving. During enlistment, applicants filled out a detailed questionnaire about their backgrounds, which included their age, schooling, work history, claimed special skills, a strip-map to their home (there are few street signs in war-ravaged Liberia), and any supporting evidence, such as certificates or diplomas. An investigator then verified the accuracy of this information; fraudulent claims and documents filed in the applications account for the majority of candidate disqualifications during the vetting process.

The first vetting method is background checks. Conducting background checks in a post-conflict country is complex and absolutely requires local knowledge. Owing to this, each investigative team comprised one Liberian and one international investigator. This team interviewed people on conditions of anonymity who knew the candidate well for character references, which included the candidate's references, neighbors, employers, co-workers, relatives, municipal authorities, teachers, community leaders, and local religious leaders (see Figure 10). To ensure interviews were controlled, confidential, and conducive to maximum disclosure, investigators tried to conduct them in private locations and use open-ended questions (e.g., "tell me about this man"). Because of the sensitive nature of investigating the past, local Liberian staff were vital as cultural interpreters and almost always accompanied the investigator. Without their support, competent investigations would not have been possible.

Figure 10. A DynCorp Vetting Team Comprising One International and One Liberian Expert Conducting Background Checks on an AFL Applicant in the Field.

Second, the vetting team ran a records check on the applicant, pooling what public records were available and prioritizing them by reliability and completeness. In its records search, DynCorp reached out to the full pantheon of neo-medieval actors in Liberia: the government of Liberia, UNMIL, and other international organizations as well as international and local NGOs.[85] The West Africa Examinations Council (WAEC) maintained some of the best identity records in the country, with thousands of Liberian identities plus photographs on file. Despite the incompleteness of the records, they helped investigators verify facts and spot forged documents and falsehoods.

Third, DynCorp conducted public vetting, a direct appeal to the population to solicit local knowledge of candidates' past wrongdoings. The candidates' pictures, names, and hometowns were publicized nationally to afford witnesses and victims an opportunity to identify undesirable candidates. Candidates were briefed of this procedure during enlistment and signed a release form authorizing DynCorp to broadcast their information. The company used posters, newspaper inserts, radio, and facebooks to disseminate the information and invited the public to provide feedback anonymously via telephone hotlines, an email address, or simply walking into an enlistment center. Additionally, some members of the public with special knowledge of past crimes, such as solicitors, academic researchers, civil society groups, and journalists, were, at times, asked to submit relevant information concerning the human rights records of persons named on the list. Not surprisingly, public vetting in Liberia attracted many false leads and fraudulent claims aimed at defaming candidates for unrelated reasons, but in a country with few public records, tapping the collective memory of the populace was an important vetting method.

Applicants could be disqualified on substantial and/or procedural grounds. Substantial reasons involve credible evidence of past wrongdoing—criminality, human rights violations, drug use, mental instability, etc.—that would be undesirable behavior in the new security forces. To this end, DynCorp compiled a list of "core crimes" that would disqualify candidates. These were drawn from crimes commonly outlawed in humanitarian and human rights law, specifically genocide, crimes against humanity, war crimes, and grave human rights abuses. Examples of core crimes include murder, rape, and torture. Individuals who were members of security units with especially bad human rights records were not dismissed categorically: All applicants received a fair investigation. Procedural grounds entailed credible evidence of wrongdoing internal to the vetting process itself, such as cheating, lying, or noncooperation in course of the investigation. In other words, substantial grounds dealt with factors external to the vetting process, while procedural grounds dealt with issues internal to the process itself. Both assessed an individual's integrity and character, and either justified the rejection of an applicant from the indigenous force.

What should be the threshold of evidence for disqualification? Theoretically, the threshold criteria for rejection of an applicant follow a simple formula: level of gravity of crime + level of evidence, balanced against other competing interests (e.g., member of an underrepresented ethnic group, applicant possesses a rare and needed skill set, etc.). Realistically, this is a tricky question and has no generalizable answer. Several standards exist for determining the quality or level of evidence, yet none are wholly satisfactory. Setting

77

standards too low results in an "open door model" that risks insurgents and criminals easily infiltrating the force. Setting them too high creates a "trial model" that would be inappropriate and protract the process.

Since vetting is used to determine an applicant's suitability for military service rather than establishing guilt or innocence of crimes, DynCorp adopted a lower standard of proof than would courts of law, disqualifying candidates based on a preponderance of evidence or "balance of probability." In other words, an applicant would be dismissed if he or she was more likely than not culpable in a crime. This standard is generally utilized for civil law trials and is widely accepted in adjudicating human rights cases, such as by the European Court of Human Rights. The "balance of probabilities" standard is an injunction to evaluate whether a given element is "more probable than not" and most suitable for SSR vetting.

When weighing the testimony of witnesses, DynCorp created a matrix that explained and ranked the trustworthiness of sources in four categories: identity, character, education, and professional experience. For each of these categories, the company gave guidelines regarding the types of persons who were most and least trustworthy. Strongly credible witnesses included people who knew the candidate well, such as a close relative or a friend who knew the candidate for 15 years or more (e.g., spouse, parent, or old friend) or people in positions of authority over the individual (e.g., high school principal, church pastor, or boss). Weak witnesses only vaguely knew the candidate; in such cases, the investigator needed to substantiate the charge with at least two or three unrelated witnesses. Allegations with few credible witnesses were generally deemed not probable and did not disqualify the applicant.

In addition to allegations of war crimes or human rights violations, histories of criminal behavior, poor reputations in the community, mental instability, and family violence, candidates could be rejected for procedural reasons that cast negative light on their suitability for soldiering. The top reasons for procedural disqualification included failure to reveal pertinent information during the procedure; evidence of threats, intimidation, or coercion of victims, references, or witnesses; lack of cooperation with or support for the vetting process; or aggressive, violent, insulting, or disrespectful behavior toward staff. In the first 6 months of recruiting and vetting, 1,080 candidates were investigated; of these, 335 were accepted and 205 were rejected, almost all for procedural rather than substantive reasons. This may be because the recruiting campaign stressed the need for candidates free of criminal or human rights violations in their background, and thus the applicant pool was self-selecting. It may also be because procedural problems were easier to unearth than substantive ones.

Importantly, DynCorp did not admit or dismiss any applicant based on vetting: This was the job of the Joint Personnel Board (JPB). Once a candidate passed all recruiting requirements and completed the vetting process, DynCorp scored their merit based on how well they did in each category, ranked them on an order of merit list, and then passed the candidate's file to the JPB. Three individuals comprised the JPB: a member of the Liberian government (appointed by the Minister of Defence), a member of Liberian civil society (also appointed by the Minister of Defence), and a U.S. Embassy official. After the JPB reviewed the applicant's file, test results, and vetting findings, it then voted on whether to admit the candidate into the new AFL as a recruit. A simple majority won. Rejected applicants could appeal to a similarly constructed Joint Review Board (JRB), which had final determining authority. Recruits spent the first year of their service on probation, during which their performances were evaluated. At the end of this first year, the JPB convened to decide whether to retain or dismiss the soldier. UNMIL could observe the process but had no vote. DynCorp only acted as the administrative facilitator and also had no vote.

The recruiting and vetting campaign was fairly effective, given the high enlistment rate in the first 6 months of recruiting. DynCorp received 4,170 applicants in the first 6 months of recruiting. The average age was 29 years, and there was a fairly even dispersion of tribal group. No single group accounted for more than 12 percent of the applicant pool, although some groups represented less than 1 percent, such as Sarpo, Bella, and Dei.[86] No one was identified as Americo-Liberian or Congo, though .8 percent did not select a group on the enlistment application form, which asks individuals to identify their tribe rather than ethnic group. Neither Americo-Liberians nor Congo regard themselves as a tribe.

Two-thirds of all applicants resided in the county of Montserrado, where Monrovia is located, though because the war drove most of Liberia's population to its capital, this should not be interpreted as reflecting applicants' counties of origin. Most candidates were born in Montserrado (22 percent), Lofa (16 percent), or Nimba (14 percent), while the fewest came from River Gee (2 percent), Gbarpolu (1 percent), and Rivercess (1 percent). In general, the applicants were representative of the population, consistent with the DoS and the Liberian government's desire for an ethnically balanced military.

Curiously, only 772 applicants, or 18.5 percent of the applicant pool, claimed former military experience, either in the AFL or a rebel group. No doubt some withheld this information when applying, especially during the early days of recruitment when the SSR program's reputation was still inchoate. Over half of these applicants claimed they served in the AFL, with the remainder more or less evenly divided among former LURD, MODEL, militia, and the National Patriotic Front of Liberia, a rebel group led by Taylor during the First Liberian Civil War from 1989 to 1996. A small number of candidates claimed they served in special units created by Taylor towards the end of the war that terrorized the population and enemy alike, such as the Special Operations Division and Special Secret Service. No applicant was denied entry into the new AFL because they were part of a notorious unit; candidates were only rejected when background checks revealed participation in human rights violations or crimes. Applicants with former military experience scored substantially lower on vetting benchmarks than applicants without former military experience.

Both the Liberian government and the DoS had asked DynCorp to emphasize female recruitment, and in 2006, Johnson-Sirleaf astonishingly declared that 20 percent of all soldiers in the AFL should be women, perhaps the highest percentage of women in any military.[87] DynCorp correspondingly held women-only recruitment days, featured women soldiers in comics and billboards, and hired female veterans of the old AFL's Women Auxiliary Corps to staff the AFL information booth in downtown Monrovia. Despite these efforts, only 130 of the 4,170 applicants were female, constituting 3.2 percent of the applicant pool. When asked, one woman said she did not want to join the military because it would make her "muscly" and "no man wants a woman muscly." When it was pointed out to her that she—and many women in Liberia—walked several miles a day with a few gallons of water or a sack of rice balanced on their head yet remained "unmuscly," she simply grinned and left.[88]

Vetting is an area where the objectives of post-conflict security and justice can clash. Key to the success of the vetting program was guaranteeing the anonymity of people who gave information about applicants. Failure to protect the identities of witnesses and victims of crimes invited reprisals and even death: With a feeble judiciary and scant law enforcement, violence was never far beneath the surface. However, this was controversial because it meant that vetting must remain absolutely unconnected to instruments of post-conflict justice, such as a truth commission or a war crimes tribunal.

This became an issue in the summer of 2006 when Liberia's nascent Truth and Reconciliation Commission (TRC) demanded all of DynCorp's vetting records for transitional justice purposes. By this time, DynCorp had amassed one of the most complete sets of records on individuals in the country, especially regarding ex-combatants. Causing controversy within UNMIL, DynCorp refused to hand over its records, since it would reveal the identities of witnesses as well as vetting sources and methods. If the TRC were to use the vetting records as evidence, making them public in the process or leaking them by accident, it would invite reprisals against the witnesses and also compromise the AFL SSR program, since no one would volunteer to join if they thought it would land them in front of the TRC. The objective of vetting is to assess suitability for service in a security force; it is not about determining guilt or innocence, and consequently should be disassociated from transitional justice efforts.

Clearly, it is desirable that potential perpetrators of violence be brought before the TRC. However, sometimes in volatile situations like post-conflict Liberia, the needs of transitional justice and security are at odds with each other, and leaders must choose between the two. The real tragedy is that the choice must be made at all, as Liberians deserve both. At the time, the immediate needs of security outweighed the need for transitional justice. As a PMC, it was easier for DynCorp to refuse the TRC than for the U.S. Government to do so, since the United States does not wish to be publically portrayed as retarding post-conflict justice, even when it is, at times, necessary. This may be an instance when plausible deniability afforded by private companies serves the employer's interests.

Now that the SSR program is complete, the Liberian government could choose to release the vetting records. As long as the TRC is not politicized, such an action could prove an important confidence building measure for the public and the AFL's final step in becoming a full-fledged transparent army governed by civilian authorities and accountable to the rule of law. It would help dispel mistrust that the records are being concealed to protect the guilty, and that this AFL was truly "new," removing the taint of the civil war once and for all.

Step 4: Training and Equipping.

Training and equipping the force is the simplest part of building an army. Although military training varies from place to place, the principles involved in transforming civilians into soldiers are so time-less that they are practically clichés: intense physical conditioning and psychological hardening; breaking down individual egos and building them back up as a unit; bonding through mutual suffering; the more the recruits sweat in peace, the less they bleed in war; repetitive drills until soldiers can literally accomplish military tasks in their sleep. The foundational document of U.S. Army training—and now AFL training—is *U.S. Army Regulation 350-1: Army Training and Leader Development (AR 350-1)*. DynCorp adopted the U.S. Army's initial entry training (IET) program for the AFL's basic training, modifying it for the needs of Liberia, and hired only ex-U.S. Army and Marine drill sergeants (see Figure 11) to transform the recruits into soldiers.[89]

**Figure 11. AFL Basic Training with a
DynCorp Drill Sergeant.**

Grounded in AR 350-1, DynCorp planned four training courses for the AFL. Basic training—that is, IET—initially lasted 15 weeks but later was reduced due to lack of funding. Following this, recruits would undergo advanced individual training (AIT), which usually lasted 6 weeks and provided specialized training to soldiers based on their military occupation speciality (MOS), such as infantry, medic, or cook. Every member of the AFL undertook IET and AIT, but soldiers selected for leadership underwent additional training. Those selected as noncommissioned officers (NCOs, also known as sergeants) attended a basic NCO course (BNCOC, pronounced *bee-knock*) for 4 weeks, and those selected as officers attended an officer basic course (OBC) for 6 weeks. Rather than examine each of these courses in depth, it may prove more useful to analyze one course, basic training, because it was the most widely attended and illustrates how DynCorp adapted U.S. military training to the AFL's unique needs.

The original basic training program was revolutionary. Early planners at DynCorp believed that after 14 years of civil war, most Liberians knew how to fire an AK-47 but did not know when or at what. Thus, the original basic training curriculum and first iteration reduced the number of hours AFL recruits spent on the range and added 3 weeks' worth of civics classes, which taught the laws of war, ethics, and the like. The curriculum was designed in partnership with Liberian lawyers, historians, and educators, as well as DynCorp staff with backgrounds in international public law and military training. The 120 hours of civics instruction dwarfed all other training, with basic rifle marksmanship (BRM) coming in a distant second at under 50 hours. The firm also partnered with international NGOs such as the International Committee of the Red Cross (ICRC) to deliver 8 hours of instruction on international humanitarian law and human rights. At the time, the volume of civics instruction was unprecedented in modern militaries, but few modern militaries face the challenges of the AFL.

Additionally, the civics instruction addressed vital concerns of the AFL such as federalism. As in most fragmented states, people in Liberia often identified first with their tribe and second with their state, which had corrupted the national military. As mentioned previously, Doe had replaced much of the AFL leadership with members of his Krahn tribe, turning the military into a sectarian war machine in the 1980s. To avoid this in the future, the Liberian government and the DoS demanded that DynCorp create an AFL with balanced ethnic representation in the ranks and also a strong national identity that superseded tribal loyalty. To answer its client's demands, DynCorp dedicated significant time in the civics section to Liberian history, loyalty to the constitution, organization of the Liberian government, the civil-military relationship, the rule of law, and other topics that imbued a national consciousness and duty to state above all else.[90] Designed and often delivered by Liberian professional educators, this curriculum aspired to engender respect for federalism within the ranks.

Another key challenge facing the AFL was literacy. Military leaders and ideally the entire force would be literate. But Liberia's high illiteracy rate, combined with Taylor's denial of education to his tribal enemies during the war, meant that some ethnic groups were less literate than others. This created a conundrum, since the DoS gave DynCorp the dual mandate of a literate and ethnically balanced military. To overcome this, DynCorp accepted some candidates from minority groups with lower literacy rates and embedded a literacy program into basic training for any recruit wanting or needing it.

Infusing civics, federalism, and literacy instruction into the overall basic training framework is an excellent example of private sector innovation not found in similar public sector efforts. U.S. efforts at raising security forces in Afghanistan, Iraq, and Mali faced similar hurdles as were seen in Liberia, yet lacked any sort of systematic approach to instilling federalism, literacy, or respect for the rule of law.

This failure stems, in part, from the U.S. military's reluctance to abandon its doctrine when restructuring security forces, often to the detriment of those foreign forces—and unfortunately, like the market for force in the Middle Ages, the contractor is only as good as the client. After the first iteration of basic training, the DoS asked DynCorp to remove the 3 weeks of civics courses on advice from the DoD and to save money. Therefore, it is difficult to assess the efficacy of DynCorp's civics program.

To save money, the DoS chose to shorten basic training by 3 weeks, which it did by removing all civics, human rights, and laws of war classes—perhaps the most important training for the new AFL, since most recruits already knew how to shoot an AK-47 from the war. Industry critics might find this surprising, naturally assuming that the DoS would want the civics curriculum and that the PMC would have no interest in implementing it, which if true, would have been a classic case of the profit motive overriding policy concerns.

In terms of equipping the recruits, conflict-zone logistics is the private military industry's forte, as contractors manage the majority of DoD logistics requirements around the world. DynCorp's team of ex-military and civilian logisticians at the company's offices in Dallas equipped the AFL through the global supply chain. Since Liberia was under a strict UN arms embargo at the time, the DoS and DynCorp worked together closely in 2006 to purchase small arms in Eastern Europe and fly the weapons to Liberia via chartered cargo plane. To minimize ambush by clandestine rebel groups, the planes landed unannounced in the dead of night. The DoS arranged an exemption to the UN arms embargo, over-flight permissions, end user certificates, and money for the operation. DynCorp found the supplier, transacted the deal, and moved the weapons from Eastern Europe to Liberia. The deal was the first legal arms transaction to Liberia in nearly 2 decades.

Step 5: Strategy and Institutional Support.

It takes more than soldiers and weapons to make an army. Therefore, DynCorp was also contracted to demobilize and rebuild the Ministry of Defence to develop defense strategy and manage the AFL's human resources, public affairs, resource management, ombudsman, coordination with other ministries, and other vital functions. Because ministries of defense in fragile states are often bloated affairs, the DoS directed the company to create a lean organization of about 100 people, almost all civilians and led by a civilian minister. Once AFL recruiting and training was underway, DynCorp undertook the creation of a small military civil service.

Rebuilding a ministry is far from a facile affair. Public sector militaries like the U.S. Army generally do not conduct institutional reform, as it is not seen as a core military function. Instead, development agencies such as USAID or the World Bank typically assist host nations with the work. However, development organizations are often prohibited from working with military institutions or shun doing so, and consequently transforming a ministry of defense in particular remains largely unmapped territory.[91] This did not deter DynCorp, which sought out relevant experts and lured them to Liberia through competitive pay packages in a manner no state bureaucracy can afford or has the flexibility to accommodate. Because practice was ahead of theory in 2005, many of the experts were retired U.S. military officers and defense attachés with substantial experience working with African ministries of defense.

Within months, the firm formed a 20-person team that devised a 17-week civil servant training course divided into 10 functional areas, followed by 16 weeks of on-the-job mentorship.[92] The team also would help the fledgling Liberian ministry draft all plans, policies, and procedures for the AFL—a major task—as well as assist in formulating military strategy. Unfortunately, this plan never came to fruition due to contractual pay problems, so it is impossible to assess its effectiveness, although it could serve as a useful model for future efforts. Today the Ministry of Defence has mostly learned by doing, a less than ideal approach to ministerial development.

One interesting aspect of hiring a private company to conduct SSR rather than the DoD is that DynCorp was not beholden to any country's military doctrine or textbook solutions. Instead, it could freely mold existing protocols without fear of institutional reprisal. Substantially modifying doctrine to fit the needs of a host nation is a departure from the U.S. practice, which, as recent experience suggests, tends to transpose — wholesale — its own military models onto foreign forces without consideration as to whether they are appropriate or not. Not surprisingly, these efforts meet limited success: U.S. solutions to Iraqi or Afghani problems have made for a poor fit. By contrast, in Liberia, DynCorp used U.S. Army training doctrine as a baseline for innovation rather than as an outright solution.

Additionally, DynCorp's bureaucratic outsider status allowed it to support Liberia's interests in the back offices of the Pentagon and the DoS in Washington, DC, where Liberians could seldom venture. It became evident during the consultations that Liberians strongly advocated gender equality in the ranks, while the U.S. Government did not. Before the civil war, the AFL had an all-female unit called the Women's Auxiliary Corps, which was well respected even in 2005, and during the civil war, some of the most feared warlords, such as Black Diamond, were women. Liberians understood that women could be effective warriors. However, until recently the U.S. military held that women were not fit for combat and therefore should not serve in front-line units, and it initially opposed including women in AFL infantry units.

DynCorp thus became an unwitting arbitrator in a debate between the defense establishments in Washington, DC, and Monrovia. As a nominal outsider in the process, DynCorp could credibly present ideas and recommendations to entrenched bureaucracies on both sides of the Atlantic without the burdens of institutional loyalty or prejudice. This helped drive the argument for gender parity, since key managers in DynCorp were persuaded by the Liberians' case.

Because the DoS managed the SSR contract, it had the final vote on the matter and opted for gender parity, overruling the DoD desire to use U.S. military templates and its bias against women in infantry units. Consequently, Liberian women may now enjoy greater equality in their military than do American women.

By 2010, Liberia had a small fledgling army and, in 2013, it is preparing to possibly deploy to Mali for a peacekeeping mission, 10 years after Charles Taylor fled Liberia, and the AFL was widely viewed as a cause of conflict. It remains a qualified success compared to efforts in Afghanistan, Iraq, East Timor, Côte d'Ivoire, and elsewhere where new security forces degenerated into sectarian killing machines or coup d'etat makers. One of the features that makes Liberia unique is that a PMC raised its army, revealing some of the good, bad, and ugly implications of today's private military industry and the future of DDR and SSR, since many of these programs will likely be outsourced in the future.

Other Challenges.

As with any complex contingency operations, few things went as planned. Two especially difficult challenges for the operator on the ground are discussed.

Erratic Funding.

The United States paid for the SSR program, except for the soldiers' salaries, making progress vulnerable to the ebb and flow of DoS funding.[93] Money for the DDR of 13,770 legacy soldiers was scarce, delaying their demobilization and placing the entire SSR effort—and arguably the country—in peril. In late April 2006, 400 to 500 former AFL soldiers conducted a violent protest outside the Ministry of Defence, claiming nonpayment of salary arrears and retirement benefits, and clashed with UNMIL peacekeepers sent to quell the unrest.[94]

Erratic funding to other parts of the program resulted in inchoate outcomes. The Ministry of Defence reform program was prematurely terminated after the completion of a 17-week civil servant training course but before the implementation of a planned 5-month mentoring and on-the-job training phase. Consequently, new civil servants had no source of advice or assistance as they assumed their official duties in the new ministry, rendering it severely incapacitated.[95]

Lapses in client funding and Liberian capacity also created dangerous situations. Training was stopped for months due to lack of payment by the DoS, leaving new soldiers to sit idle while they waited for follow-on recruits to fill out their units. Making matters worse, the Ministry of Finance still did not have the capacity to pay soldiers in 2006, demonstrating that in recovering failed states, all institutions must work together. This created the dangerous situation of unpaid and disgruntled soldiers that the SSR program sought to avoid from the outset.

Meanwhile, those ready to report to basic training were literally told, "Don't call us, we'll call you," by frustrated SSR program staff. The program then consisted of nearly 100 international (U.S. and third-country national personnel combined) and several hundred local national staff. Sending the international staff home and furloughing the local staff to save money would cause resentment among the locals, given Liberia's 75 percent unemployment rate, and many of the international staff were specialists who were difficult to replace.

Frustrated and fearing that it might have to leave Liberia for lack of payment—an option few public armies would consider—DynCorp urged its client to stabilize the funding stream. The high cost of paying expensive employees to sit idle in a country where the average person subsisted on $1.25 a day sent a cynical message to the population, already somewhat dubious over the new AFL. Also, it created a dangerous situation in an unstable state, as DynCorp was unable to store weapons and ammunition safely without an armory, which PA&E was scheduled to build but could not, because of lack of money. Worse, soldiers who completed training would have no military base to report to, as PA&E had yet to complete bases. This could prove a perilous situation for Liberian society and discredit the entire SSR program. As Mark Malan noted, "Weak and erratic funding from the U.S. Department of State is the main cause of the slow pace of AFL development."[96]

Local Ownership and Contractors.

"Local ownership" has become a mantra in the international development community; it refers to local political and popular support for foreign assistance programs like SSR, and there is a growing consensus among scholars that early local ownership is crucial to program sustainability and legitimacy.[97] The concept is simple enough: A foreign power that wields a heavy hand in transforming another country will likely alienate the very people it aspires to benefit, negating the purpose of the program. Or, as Laurie Nathan explains, "Experience shows that reform processes will not succeed in the absence of commitment and ownership on the part of those undertaking reforms."[98]

Because the AFL SSR process relied heavily on U.S. support, some scholars assert it lacks ownership, sustainability, and legitimacy.[99] Morten Bøås and Kari-anne Stig sum up this collective critique when they claim that the lack of transparency, accountability, and participation of local Liberians in the SSR process led to a paucity of ownership of the program.[100] Even the U.S. Congressional Research Service questions the balance between foreign support for and national ownership of security in Liberia and worries that lack of adequate public input has created an AFL where "political legitimacy might be called into question."[101]

Contractors compound the quandary of ownership because, as Adedeji Ebo reasons, "There is no direct contractual obligation between the security contractor and the institutions and people of the reforming state."[102] Not even the Liberian Minister of Defence had a copy of DynCorp's contract to transform the AFL he was to lead, demonstrating a lack of transparency in the process. This created a problematic situation. Liberians were neither an employer nor a signatory to the contract, even though they were the intended beneficiaries of the program. Consequently, the Liberian government had only limited ability to direct DynCorp; the company, in essence, was not accountable to the state, even as it was rebuilding its military forces. For Bøås and Stig, "This clearly represents a democratic deficit in the SSR."[103]

However, critics' conclusions may be overstated. Few Liberians seemed concerned about the U.S. role in the AFL SSR process, especially given the urgent need for military reform and the strong historical ties between the two countries. Nor were Liberians troubled by the presence of contractors: There were no riots, protests, violence, or other evidence of widespread

PMC rejection. DynCorp's frequent overtures to civil society—almost always through the government of Liberia—were met with general disinterest. The Liberian Minister of Defence had multiple occasions to join DynCorp on its recruitment trips starting in 2006, but chose not to accompany the firm until 2008.[104] Additionally, the NTGL—and not DynCorp—determined who was eligible for demobilization benefits and who would be admitted into the new AFL. This indicates a lack of worry on the Liberian government's part rather than a failure of transparency on DynCorp's, as more recent scholarship confirms:

> The Liberian Ministry of Defence, the legislature and civil society have had opportunities to involve themselves more in the reform than they have done, thus suggesting that the reform is not proceeding as such a closed process as previous research on the SSR has argued.[105]

Other problems undermine academic critiques over ownership. Can foreign scholars really speak for Liberians on the question of local ownership? Can outside observers claim Liberia had no ownership of AFL SSR if its government had approved and accepted a gratis program that the United States provided through its contractors?[106] Can simultaneous assertions that there was no local ownership and that ownership is necessary for success be made if Liberians have not rejected the AFL, and it is a success compared to the Liberian National Police and other elements of the security sector? On this last point, the ICG describes progress in Liberia's security sector reform as "uneven": While "the police are still widely considered ineffective and corrupt. . . . Army reform appears to be a provisional success."[107]

Other researchers are more harsh in their critique of contractors in Liberia, inferring that they are mercenaries. As Malan writes, "In a country and region where recent history has been shaped by warlords and mercenaries, the U.S. Department of State has shown remarkable insensitivity by sending in contractors to shape the new army."[108] Unfortunately, Malan offers no further explanation or support for this serious claim. Comparing DynCorp to Liberian warlords and mercenaries without supporting evidence is irresponsible and absurd.

The concept of local "ownership" sits well among academics and policymakers, but the reality on the ground is more nuanced: How precisely does one translate this principle into practice? What does local ownership exactly look like? How do you know when you have achieved sufficient ownership? Even the definition of local ownership is disputed: Who gets to decide who the key stakeholders are when determining local ownership? Choosing which local leaders and political groups will represent local aspirations is difficult and fraught with uncertainty, and has political ramifications both within indigenous and international politics. Also, local actors often have competing visions and priorities, and selecting local partners can be perilous in conflict-affected countries where there is often imperfect knowledge of parochial agendas. It may prove difficult to keep insurgents and spoilers out of the process, and if they are deemed key stakeholders, it provides them a platform of legitimacy and the ability to obstruct progress from within, while making it difficult to expel them. Finally, measuring ownership is difficult. What exactly does one measure? Should metrics privilege local values and priorities or international ones? Local ownership is sound in theory but nebulous in practice.

CONCLUSION

In 2003, Charles Taylor fled to Nigeria, ending a 14-year civil war that left the country post-apocalyptic and the population traumatized. It became home to the world's largest UN peacekeeping missions at the time that Nigeria began the hard work of resuscitating the country. Due to historical ties, the United States agreed to demobilize and rebuild the AFL, which was complicit in war crimes. In an interesting twist, the DoS outsourced this task to the private sector, the first time in 150 years that one sovereign hired a private company to raise another sovereign's military. This is also significant because the private sector will likely play an increasing role in building security forces in the future, making Liberia a particularly apt case study.

Liberia, and particularly the AFL, is an instructive case study of DDR and SSR since it is a qualified success. It bridges the theory and practice behind the DDR of Liberia's legacy military and SSR that built a new one. Regardless of the size of the country or the security forces—from Liberia to Afghanistan—the fundamental machinations of DDR and SSR are the same.

DDR and SSR are important because they are gateway programs. In fragile states, the construction or reconstruction of the security sector is a precondition for development, since no other reform—political, economic, or social—can take root without security. Additionally, helping failed states recover is critical to global security, since they can constitute a chronic international problem; induce regional instability; result in humanitarian tragedy; provide safe havens, training grounds, and bases of operation for global terrorists; and abet international criminal organizations that traffic in narcotics, people, small arms, terrorist skills, weapons of mass destruction, and other illicit products and services. Additionally, a competent indigenous security sector is essential for the exit strategy from costly peacekeeping missions.

Finally, as with all complex contingency operations, a certain degree of humility is required. As seen in Iraq, Afghanistan, and elsewhere, excessively ambitious visions of what is achievable often achieve little. It is far superior to start with a modest vision and build from there.

Liberia Lessons Learned.

At the International Level:

1. Political agreement. Ensure SSR and DDR have a clear mandate by including them in the peace agreement.

2. Inclusion of all warring parties. Every group that is expected to participate in DDR should be included in the peace agreement.

3. DDR and SSR are linked. They rise or fall together and should be planned, resourced, implemented, and evaluated as a single entity.

4. Comprehensive and synchronized approach. DDR and SSR require the close coordination of many agencies, such as the DoD, DoS, USAID, etc.

5. Sufficient funds and political will. Erratic support may result in a half developed security sector, which can be worse than none at all.

6. Lose the "train and equip" mentality. SSR is more than "train and equip" and involves engaging

civil society, human rights vetting, and transformation across the security sub-sectors, operational actors, institutional actors, and oversight actors. Training and equipping alone is necessary but insufficient for SSR.

Host Nation Level: Institutional Actors and Oversight Actors.

1. All politics are local. DDR and SSR are political programs because they rewire de facto authority structures in conflict affected states. Consequently, technical approaches alone will likely fail.

2. Institute security sector management. Transform institutional and oversight actors, such as ministries, perhaps even starting with these organizations.

3. Develop a sensible security strategy. Work with the host nation to develop a National Security Strategy that uniquely addresses root causes of conflict, and avoid templating other countries' strategies. In Liberia, the strategy and force structure should be focused on securing development and good governance rather than defeating foreign militaries.

4. All institutions must work together. Recognize that the army cannot get paid if the Ministry of Finance is nonoperational, as this will impact DDR and SSR success.

5. Instill, when possible, democratic principles; for example, civilian control of the military.

6. Cultivate professionalism. Transparency in oversight, accounting, promotion systems, and so forth will encourage a culture of merit.

7. Eschew ill-fitting doctrinal templates. What works for the United States may not work for the host nation.

Host Nation Level: Operational Actors.

1. Sensitize the population to what is going on. Not everyone will welcome ex-combatants into their hometowns or the creation of a new army or police force, especially if the legacy forces were complicit in crimes.

2. Spoilers. Be inclusive in planning and engage civil society, but manage spoilers effectively. If a spoiler is given a position of authority inside the program, then the DDR and SSR program may be undermined.

3. Demobilize with dignity. Combatants are more likely to cooperate if they are not treated like criminals. However, be prepared for opposition from international and domestic audiences, since many in the legacy security sector could, in fact, be criminals.

4. It may be necessary to start over. Avoid lustration and demobilize the entire force since it probably is not known who is "good" or who is "bad." UNMIL used lustration to rebuild the Liberian National Police, which was unsuccessful and remains an obstacle to stability.

5. Vigorously vet all candidates. The United States would never put a cop on the street or enlist someone for the military without a thorough background check. To not sufficiently vet individuals in conflict countries is unacceptable. Use a "balance of probabilities" standard of evidence when adjudicating applicants' files.

6. Instill professional values. Starting in basic training, instill respect for the rule of law, human rights norms and international humanitarian law, and allegiance to the constitution, rather than to an individual leader, in all training.

7. Force Structure is key. The force structure and security architecture must reflect the country's needs.

It should have a defense-oriented posture with limited force-projection capability: limited artillery, armor, intelligence, and fighter aircraft. Covert special operations units and their kindred should be avoided, since they tend to become manipulated by political factions, as was the case with police in East Timor.

8. Size is constrained by the government's ability to pay salaries. Force size should be determined by the host government's ability to pay salaries over the long term since unpaid soldiers are often a greater threat to insecurity than foreign invasion. This should be a core planning constraint when designing an SSR program.

9. A smaller, well-trained, volunteer force is preferable. It is easier to instill discipline andprofessionalism in a small force than in a larger one.

10. The force should mirror society. The new force should be inclusive of all groups, ethnicities, and women. This will help ensure it does not become a sectarian instrument of power, as the AFL was under Doe's regime. Create an ombudsman or similar office to mediate ethnic disputes within the ranks.

11. Selection for leadership is difficult. It takes 20 years to achieve the rank of colonel in the U.S. Army, yet conflict countries cannot wait that long. New forces like the AFL will initially be an "army of privates." The international partner may recommend senior leaders, but the host nation must select them. Beware of cronyism and nepotism.

12. Literacy is important. Leaders need to read and write orders. It may be necessary to include literacy courses in basic training.

13. Be aware of inherent dilemmas. For example, sometimes one must choose between security versus development. In DDR, do you grant amnesty to potential war criminals to encourage them to participate

in the program? In SSR, do you turn over vetting records to a TRC, risking reprisals against witnesses who spoke with the vetting teams? Another example: Do you prioritize ethnic inclusion or literacy? An ethnically balanced force is a guiding principle of SSR, yet in places like Liberia, some ethnic groups were denied access to education and were functionally illiterate. Building a literacy program into the training, as was the case in Liberia, helps mitigate this challenge, but such programs cannot lift an individual from a 6th to 12th grade reading level in a few months.

14. Contractors are good if you know how to manage them. DynCorp invested in innovative ideas like human security and created a unique human rights vetting program because it was not beholden to the bureaucracy and was motivated by profit to innovate. However, it may have overstepped its bounds due to poor government oversight on the ground. Harness the power of the private sector but develop the management skills to do so.

15. Lastly, be humble. SSR is a marathon and not a sprint. It involves political bargaining, operational surprises, and imperfect outcomes. Ensure expectations are managed, especially one's own.

Six Recommendations for the U.S. Army.

The U.S. Army has long been associated with Liberia's military, given the historical ties between the two countries. It helped establish the Liberia Frontier Force in 1908, Liberia's first national security force and forerunner of the AFL. Composed of 500 men and later led by American army officers, its mission was originally "to patrol the borders in the hinterland [against British and French territorial expansion] and to prevent disorder." U.S. military advisors continued to work closely with the Liberian armed forces during the interwar years and Cold War.

Despite the U.S. Army's long history of military assistance in Liberia and elsewhere, conceptual understanding of SSR remains limited, and many still view SSR activities as a second order mission. Such an approach is strategically myopic, given the expanding threat-set of transnational actors, civil war, and spillover from conflict affected states. Unless the United States wishes to deploy American boots on the ground to every strategic hot spot in the world, it needs to buttress allies' security sectors to deal with emerging problems before they become crises. DDR and SSR are tools that accomplish this, and the U.S. Army should hone these instruments since partners' land forces typically deal with most threats. Here are six recommendations that will help the U.S. Army improve this skill set.

1. Break the "train and equip" mentality regarding SSR. Historically, the U.S. Army largely treated the formation of foreign forces as a foreign internal defense (FID) mission. FID is an ill-fitting model for SSR; it is a Cold War concept informed by Maoist irregular warfare operations rather than SSR principles. In a traditional FID mission, special forces units covertly train and equip pro-American guerrillas in communist countries (e.g., the Montagnards in Vietnam) and help friendly governments defeat communist insurgents (e.g., El Salvador) in proxy wars between the United States and Soviet Union. These were essentially tactical train and equip missions that did not entail institution building, much less wholesale SSR, as is required in places like Iraq and Afghanistan. Unfortunately, many national security thinkers remain paradigm prisoners of the "train and equip" mentality, often cit-

ing as SSR progress the number of indigenous soldiers or police trained and equipped—a clever metric that never diminishes (hence insinuates progress) nor tells you anything about the quality of the security forces being produced. Training and equipping only produces better dressed soldiers who shoot straighter; it does not create an army.

2. The U.S. Army must balance its SSR efforts between operational and institutional actors. Because of the "train and equip" mentality, the military has traditionally emphasized generating indigenous "boots on the ground" at the expense of civil servants in ministries. However, an army of infantry squads without the requisite institutional backing is merely a militia. This unbalanced approach undermines the hard-won tactical gains that must be sustained by a partner state's defense institutions. Contractors are capable of filling this gap as they did in Liberia, but the U.S. Army should have an organic capacity to conduct this mission and not overly depend on the private sector to provide SSR. One promising development is the Ministry of Defense Advisors (MoDA) program. Established in 2010, it allows the U.S. Army to draw on civilian expertise to transform ministerial actors, and it should be expanded.

3. Draft mature doctrine on DDR and SSR. Currently, there are no doctrine or field manuals (FMs) dedicated to these operations despite the fact that the U.S. Army has been actively engaged in DDR and SSR undertakings in Iraq and Afghanistan for 10 years. Doctrine is needed because, as this monograph demonstrates, these are complex tasks requiring a comprehensive approach well beyond "train and equip" methodologies. Unfortunately, most SSR related doctrine remains mired in this tactical approach to SSR:

Joint Publication (JP) 3-07.1, Joint Tactics, Techniques, and Procedures for Foreign Internal Defense; U.S. Army and U.S. Marine Corps FM 3-24/MCWP3-33.5, *Counter-insurgency*, chap. 6; and *U.S. Army FM 3-07, Stability Operations*, chap. 6. After several years of FID failure in Iraq and Afghanistan, the U.S. military finally drafted more inclusive doctrine on SSR called security force assistance: *U.S. Army FM 3-07/1, Security Force Assistance*. Though a significant improvement, this model does not address the full spectrum of SSR needs, such as human rights vetting, and creates foreign militaries in the image of the U.S. Army, which is inappropriate. The U.S. Army should develop doctrine and publish a field manual dedicated to DDR and SSR as linked, modular, and scalable programs that can be tailored to unique host nation needs. Good doctrine should scope and frame ideas to make them operational and avoid what Frances Z. Brown, a development expert, terms "romantic capacity-building projects."[109]

4. Link security with justice. A U.S. congressional investigation into a $2.16 billion contract called Host Nation Trucking, which protects overland supply lines in Afghanistan, found that many subcontractors hired to provide armed protection of the trucking convoys were Afghan warlords and their militia. In some ways, this arrangement worked well: It effectively supplied most U.S. combat outposts across difficult and hostile terrain, while only rarely needing the assistance of U.S. troops. However, the report, *Warlord, Inc.*, also discovered that:

> the principal private security subcontractors on the [Host Nation Trucking] contract are warlords, strong-men, commanders and militia leaders who compete with the Afghan central government for power and authority. Providing "protection" services for the

United States supply chain empowers these warlords with money, legitimacy, and a *raison d'etre* for their private armies.[110]

Empowering local warlords, thugs, criminals, and others reviled by the local population compromises the larger aims of the mission: building a just society that upholds the rule of law. As the congressional report concluded, "The logistics contract has an outsized strategic impact on U.S. objectives in Afghanistan."[111]

5. The United States needs a Stability Police Force or similar instrument to accomplish DDR and SSR. Core to SSR is policing because it has the power to prevent conflicts, preserve social stability during crises, and support post-conflict rehabilitation. Policing is also critical for development. According to the Organization for Security and Co-operation in Europe (OSCE), "Effective policing helps create an environment where sustainable development can flourish."[112] Yet the United States lacks an expeditionary police force, probably because there is no national police force to draw from, and prefers to rely on contractors like DynCorp International for police in stability operations. But depending on contractors makes the United States overly exposed to the private sector for success in DDR and SSR. Instead, the U.S. Army should create an organic capacity by expanding the Military Police Corps to include these functions or instituting an expeditionary Stability Police Force.

6. Do no harm. On May 29, 2006, bloody riots tore through Kabul, the deadliest street violence since the defeat of the Taliban. In response, the U.S. military and Afghan authorities created an elite gendarmerie called the Afghanistan National Civil Order Police (ANCOP). The U.S. military recruited from among

the top officers currently serving in the Afghan Uniformed Police, depleting it of its best and brightest. A key criterion for selection was a 6th-grade level of literacy, an extremely high standard since more than 80 percent of the police were functionally illiterate. However, the inclusion of only literate police officers in ANCOP had unintended consequences for the overall police development program. Withdrawal of the few literate members from nearly every police unit in the country deprived those units of essential personnel. Worse, there was no way to replace this capacity since there was no force-wide literacy training program, as there was in Liberia. ANCOP soon suffered the curse of competence and was overutilized, resulting in high attrition levels and a brain drain to the overall detriment of the Afghan National Police.[113] Like war itself, building security forces is complex and risks unintended consequences.

Stability operations have become an inescapable reality of U.S. foreign policy, and key to mission success is DDR and SSR. Assisting strategic allies improve their military capabilities serves U.S. national interest because it enables partners to engage regional threats so that U.S. troops do not have to engage. Also, helping a fragile state establish the monopoly of force to uphold its rule of law strengthens it and promotes durable development, since a wanton security sector tends to devour the fruits of development. Lastly, building professional indigenous security forces is the exit strategy for costly stability operations and peacekeeping missions because it allows the host nation to secure itself.

In sum, DDR and SSR is a strategic imperative that has long been neglected despite its centrality to missions like Iraq, Afghanistan, and elsewhere. It must not remain so. The United States must develop a solid capability to build better armies, or it will remain mired in conflict affected countries like Afghanistan or face strategic surprises in places like Mali.

ENDNOTES

1. Tyrone C. Marshall, "AFRICOM Commander Addresses Concerns, Potential Solutions in Mali," *American Forces Press Service*, January 24, 2013.

2. "Green-on-Blue Blues: Afghan Soldiers Increasingly Turn on their NATO Colleagues," *The Economist*, September 1, 2012. Green indicates Afghan forces, and Blue coalition ones.

3. "Report on Progress Toward Security and Stability in Afghanistan," Washington, DC: Department of Defense, December 2012.

4. Marshall.

5. Sometimes extra "Rs" are appended to DDR for "Rehabilitation" (DDRR) or "Repatriation" (DDRRR). However, these functions are normally included in typical DDR programs. Consequently, this monograph will treat DDR as all inclusive.

6. The UN defines DDR as a process that "deals with the post-conflict security problem that arises when combatants are left without livelihoods and support networks during the vital period stretching from conflict to peace, recovery and development." See: "UN Integrated DDR Standards (IDDRS)," No. 24, New York: United Nations, available from *unddr.org/iddrs.aspx*.

7. The prisoner's dilemma is a fundamental problem in game theory that demonstrates why two people might not cooperate, even though it is in both their best interests to do so.

8. For more information on this problem, see Michael J. Dziedzic *et al.*, *Haiti: Confronting the Gangs of Port-Au-Prince*, Washington, DC: United States Institute of Peace, 2008.

9. The number of demobilized fighters (101,495) is debatably high. During the 2003 CPA talks with LURD and MODEL faction leaders, the number of combatants, including the AFL, had been put at approximately 38,000. Furthermore, less than 30,000 weapons were submitted, and the majority of DDR recipients qualified through the submission of ammunitions. Lastly, Liberians reported that widespread fraud was committed during the DDR process. See Josef Teboho Ansorge and Nana Akua Antwi-Ansorge, "Monopoly, Legitimacy, Force: DDR-SSR Liberia," Melanne Civic and Michael Miklaucic, eds., *The Monopoly of Force*, Washington, DC: NDU Press, 2011, pp. 265-284.

10. John Blaney *et al.*, "Wider Lessons for Peacebuilding: Security Sector Reform in Liberia," Policy Analysis Brief, Muscatine, IA: The Stanley Foundation, 2010, p. 5.

11. SSR theory is generally conceived by academics, human rights lawyers, and international development specialists who produce normative SSR frameworks espousing human rights, democracy, and sometimes a near-utopian end state for the world's most dangerous places. To achieve this SSR vision, the UN, donor states, and a pantheon of global actors involved in SSR must work together in a holistic and seamless manner, and will require, as Mark Sedra explains, "a radical change in the modus operandi of donor states in how they provide assistance" (p. 17). For examples of this SSR approach, see Mark Sedra, ed. *The Future of Security Sector Reform*, Waterloo, Canada: The Centre for International Governance Innovation, 2010, and its authors; Organisation for Economic Co-operation and Development and Development Assistance Committee *et al.*, *The OECD DAC Handbook on Security System Reform: Supporting Security and Justice*, Paris: France, OECD, 2007. Such a vision is impracticable. Absent from this idealization are the voices of practitioners, such as military professionals, who are often too busy in the field to attend academic conferences on SSR. Unfortunately, they tend to treat SSR as a train-and-equip exercise and ignore its other vital roles, which is equally untenable, as demonstrated by U.S. efforts in Iraq and Afghanistan. See *Joint Publication (JP) 3-07.1, Joint Tactics, Techniques, and Procedures for Foreign Internal Defense (FID)*, April 30, 2004, available from *www.dtic.mil/cgi-bin/GetTRDoc?AD=ADA434396& Location=U2&doc=GetTRDoc.pdf*; *U.S. Army and U.S. Marine Corps,*

FM 3-24/MCWP 3-33.5: Counterinsurgency, chap. 6; *U.S. Army FM 3-07.1: Security Force Assistance*, Washington, DC: Headquarters, Department of the Army, 2009. Some theorists have challenged the orthodox theory of SSR and advocate for pragmatic SSR that deals with discrete elements of the security sector, occupying a middle ground between the sweeping all-or-nothing approach of academic idealists and the narrow train-and-equip thinking of practitioners. See Eric Scheye, "Realism and Pragmatism in Security Sector Development," Paris, France: OECD, 2010.

12. Attempts have been made to formalize and operationalize SSR best practices, but serious problems persist. For one, SSR is a complex process that requires the close integration of security and development organizations, yet most attempts to conceive SSR are conducted by either security or development agencies, but not both. The result is conceptual incoherence. Security organizations tend to fold SSR into combat doctrine under the nebulous rubric of stability operations. For example, the U.S. Army devotes but a single chapter to this complex topic in both *FM 3-24, Counterinsurgency*, and *FM 3-07, Stability Operations*, and only discusses abstract principles of SSR rather than operationalizing the idea, which is the singular purpose of military field manuals. Similarly, development agencies tend to propagate legalistic and donor-oriented methods, focusing on standards and norms rather than advancing concrete methods or strategies for conducting SSR on the ground. See, *OECD DAC Handbook on Security Sector Reform*. To date, neither the UN nor any other international organization, NGO, or country has developed a comprehensive approach to SSR capable of being operationalized.

13. For an explanation of "ends, ways, and means" as a strategic construct, see Mackubin Thomas Owens, "Strategy and the Strategic Way of Thinking," *Naval War College Review*, Vol. 60, No. 4, 2007, pp. 111-124; Harry R. Yarger, "Towards A Theory of Strategy: Art Lykke and the Army War College Strategy Model," J. Boone Bartholomees, ed., *Guide to National Security Policy and Strategy. Volume I: Theory of War and Strategy*, Carlisle, PA: Strategic Studies Institute, U.S. Army War College, 2008, pp. 43-49.

14. In military parlance, a "force structure" is the organization and hierarchy of units within an army, from the general staff down to the basic infantry squad. It is similar to a massive organi-

zational chart for an army, and it outlines how military personnel, weapons and equipment are organized for the operations.

15. This table serves only as an example, as every security sector is unique, although most have a military, police, and other elements.

16. For more information on this topic, see Liz Panarelli, "Local Ownership of Security Sector Reform," Peace Report, Washington, DC: United States Institute of Peace, 2009; Marc J. Cohen and Tara R. Gingerich, *Protect and Serve or Train and Equip? U.S. Security Assistance and Protection of Civilians*, Washington, DC: Oxfam America, 2009.

17. It remains unclear how operational human security is. How exactly should a military guarantee "freedom from fear" and "freedom from want," a twin mandate of human security? See the 1994 UNDP report that popularized the human security concept and borrows these phrases from U.S. President Franklin D. Roosevelt's famous Four Freedoms speech of 1941, in which freedom from want is characterized as the third, and freedom from fear the fourth fundamental and universal freedom. See United Nations Development Program (UNDP), "New Dimensions of Human Security," Human Development Report 1994, New York: Oxford University Press, 1994, p. 3.

18. The concept of a monopoly on the use of force or violence is derived from German sociologist Max Weber's classic definition of the state as "a human community that claims the monopoly of the legitimate use of physical force within a given territory." See Max Weber, "Politics as a Vocation," Hans Heinrich Gerth and C. Wright Mills, eds. and trans., *From Max Weber: Essays in Sociology*, New York: Oxford University Press, 1958, p. 77.

19. See, e.g., Camille Conaway and Salome Martinez, *Adding Value: Women's Contributions to Reintegration and Reconstruction in El Salvador*, Washington, DC: Hunt Alternatives, 2004; Megan Bastick and Kristin Valasek, eds., *Gender and Security Sector Reform Toolkit*, Geneva, Switzerland: DCAF, OSCE/ODIHR, and UN-INSTRAW, 2008.

20. Notable exceptions include Atsushi Yasutomi, "Linking DDR and SSR in Post-conflict States: Agendas for Effective Security Sector Reintegration," *Central European Journal of International and Security Studies*, Vol. 3, Issue 2, May 2008; Owen Greene and Simon Rynn, "Linking and Coordinating DDR and SSR for Human Security after Conflict: Issues, Experience and Priorities," Working Paper 2, Stanford, CA: Stanford University, Center for International Cooperation and Security, July 2008; Michael Brzoska, "Embedding DDR Programme In Security Sector Reconstruction," Alan Bryden and Heiner Hanggi, eds., *Security Governance in Post-Conflict Peacebuilding*, London, UK: Geneva Centre for the Democratic Control of Armed Forces (DCAF)/Transaction Publishers, 2005, p. 104; Alan Bryden, "Understanding The DDR-SSR Nexus: Building Sustainable Peace in Africa," Second International Conference On DDR and Stability in Africa, Kinshasa, Democratic Republic of Congo, June12–14, 2007 (OSAA/DRC), Issue paper, June 2007; Jeremy Ginifer, "Support For DDR and SSR After Conflicts in Africa: Lessons Learnt and New Agendas in Africa, Conflict Prevention, Management and Reduction in Africa," Paper 3, A joint project of the Finnish Institute of International Affairs and the Centre for International Cooperation and Security, Helsinki, Finland: Ministry for Foreign Affairs of Finland, 2007; Multi-Country Demobilization and Reintegration Program (MDRP) Secretariat, "Linkages between Disarmament, Demobilization and Reintegration of Ex-Combatants and Security Sector Reform," October 2003.

21. See, e.g., United Nations Disarmament, Demobilization, and Reintegration Resource Centre (UNDDR), UN Integrated DDR Standards (IDDRS), available from *unddr.org/iddrs.aspx;* Organization for Economic Cooperation and Development–Development Assistance Committee (OECD-DAC), OECD DAC *Handbook on Security System Reform*, Paris, France: OECD, 2007, available from *oecd-ilibrary.org/development/the-oecd-dac-handbook-on-security-system-reform_9789264027862-en*.

22. Many members of the AFL remained in their barracks and did not partake in the fighting. Not everyone in the AFL supported Taylor.

23. Quoted in William Reno, "Reinvention of an African Patrimonial State: Charles Taylor's Liberia," *Third World Quarterly*, Vol. 16, No. 1, 1995, p. 109.

24. Sixth Annual Report of the President of the Special Court for Sierra Leone, Freetown, Sierra Leone: Special Court For Sierra Leone, 2009.

25. Interview with an ex-combatant, Monrovia, Liberia, May 12, 2004. Other accounts of gruesome acts from eyewitnesses include human heads on chairs and tables in the middle of the road as a warning to others; stringing human entrails across concertina wire to make an ad hoc road block at which cars would be stopped and robbed and perhaps passengers raped or killed; combatants would capture a pregnant woman, bet on the gender of her baby, and then find out.

26. "The World's Worst: Liberia," *The Economist*, 2002.

27. John Blaney, interview by Ky Luu, Disaster Resilience Leadership Academy, YouTube Upload, September 11, 2009, available from *www.youtube.com/watch?v=cdGGs6QGaCU*.

28. "U.S. Military Experts Confront Carnage in Liberia," *Associated Press*, July 9, 2003.

29. *Ibid.*

30. According to a 1963 Pan American (Pan Am) airlines brochure describing Liberia, "Tourists are welcome here and are treated with great friendliness and courtesy. The coastal area on the Atlantic Ocean has beautiful beaches and good fishing." See Matt Jones, "Moved2Monrovia," available from *3.bp.blogspot. com/_nAWhnWKWr-w/THZicXetaMI/AAAAAAAAAoc/qqZrx-kx-qY0/s1600/PANAM+LIBERIA.jpg*.

31. Scott Lindlaw, "Bush Approves Small Peacekeeping Contingent for Liberia," *Associated Press*, July 6, 2003.

32. "Transcript: U.S. Debating Sending Troops to Help Liberian Civil War," CNN, July 2, 2003. However, in March 2006, Nigeria handed Taylor over to Liberian authorities for trial, who in turn handed him over to the Special Court for Sierra Leone. This court was set up jointly by the government of Sierra Leone and the UN to try those most responsible for serious violations of interna-

tional humanitarian law during the civil war there (1991–2002). See Stephen Faris, "War Returns to Monrovia," *Time Magazine*, July 20, 2003; Sixth Annual Report of the President of the Special Court for Sierra Leone.

33. UN Security Council (S/RES/1497 [2003]), "Resolution 1497 (2003): Adopted by the Security Council at Its 4803rd Meeting, on 1 August 2003," August 1, 2003, available from *securitycouncilreport.org/atf/cf/%7B65BFCF9B-6D27-4E9C-8CD3-CF6E4FF96FF9%7D/UNRO%20SRES%201497.pdf*.

34. Stephan Faris, "Charles Taylor Leaves Liberia," *Time Magazine*, August 11, 2003.

35. Glenn Mckenzie, "Rebels Lift Siege of Liberia's Starving Capital, U.S. Marines Land," *The Associated Press*, August 14, 2003; "Rebels Lift Siege of Starving Monrovia," *RedOrbit.com*, August 14, 2003, available from *www.redorbit.com/news/general/14811/rebels_lift_siege_of_starving_monrovia/*.

36. "Comprehensive Peace Agreement Between the Government of Liberia and the Liberians United for Reconciliation and Democracy (LURD) and the Movement for Democracy in Liberia (MODEL) and Political Parties," August 18, 2003, available from *www.usip.org/files/file/resources/collections/peace_agreements/liberia_08182003.pdf*.

37. "Overview of Activities in Liberia," Washington, DC: United States Agency for International Development, May 4, 2004.

38. International Monetary Fund, "Liberia: Interim Poverty Reduction Strategy Paper," Washington, DC: IMF, 2007, p. x; IDP Advisory Team Policy Development and Evaluation Service, "Real-Time Evaluation of UNHCR's IDP Operation in Liberia," Geneva, Switzerland: United Nations High Commissioner for Refugees (UNHCR), 2007, p. 7; UNHCR, "Liberia: Regional Operations Profile - West Africa," available from *www.unhcr.org/cgi-bin/texis/vtx/page?page=49e484936#*; International Committee of the Red Cross (ICRC), "Liberia: Opinion Survey and in-Depth Research," Geneva, Switzerland: ICRC, 2009, p. 1. For more on the significance of the data, especially in post-conflict Liberia, see Josef Teboho Ansorge, "The Technics of Politics: Information Tech-

nology in International Relations," doctoral book, Cambridge, UK: University of Cambridge, 2011, pp. 205-225.

39. J. Peter Pham, *Liberia: Portrait of a Failed State*, Gainesville, GA: Reed Press, 2004, p. 191.

40. Robin Dunn-Marcos *et al.*, *The Liberians: An Introduction to Their History and Culture*, Washington, DC: Center for Applied Linguistics, 2005, p. 9.

41. Pham, p. 7.

42. Stephen Ellis, *The Mask of Anarchy: The Destruction of Liberia and the Religious Roots of an African Civil War*, London, UK: Hurst & Co Ltd, 2001, p. 63; Reed Kramer, "Liberia: A Casualty of the Cold War's End," *Africa Notes*, Washington, DC: Center for Strategic and International Studies (CSIS), July 1995, p. 3.

43. *Ibid.*, p. 59.

44. "Liberia: Interim Poverty Reduction Strategy Paper," p. x; "Real-Time Evaluation of UNHCR's IDP Operation in Liberia," p. 7; "Liberia: Regional Operations Profile — West Africa"; "Liberia: Opinion Survey and in-Depth Research," p. 1.

45. In 2009, Liberia's Truth and Reconciliation Commission listed President Ellen Johnson-Sirleaf as one of 52 people who should be sanctioned for committing war crimes but then retracted the report just hours before publication on its website. See Glenna Gordon, "In Liberia, Sirleaf's Past Sullies Her Clean Image," *Time Magazine*, July 3, 2009; Kate Thomas, "Liberia Truth and Reconciliation Commission Retracts Controversial Report," *Voice of America*, July 2, 2009.

46. Douglas Farah and Stephen Braun, *Merchant of Death: Money, Guns, Planes, and the Man Who Makes War Possible*, Hoboken, NJ: John Wiley & Sons, Inc., 2007, p. 167.

47. David Crane, "Press Release: Statement on International Women's Day," Special Court for Sierra Leone - The Office of the Prosecutor, Freetown, Sierra Leone, March 8, 2003.

48. "U.S. Ambassador to Liberia Urges Rebels to Leave Capital," *The New York Times*, July 28, 2003.

49. On February 27, 2007, Bryant was charged with embezzlement. His government is alleged to have stolen at least $1 million at a time when the annual gross national income per capita was $116 (2011 U.S.$). See Joseph Winter, "Africa - New Front in Drugs War," BBC News, July 9, 2007. Data from "Liberia," United Nations Statistics Division, available from *data.un.org/CountryProfile.aspx?crName=Liberia*.

50. Blaney *et al.*

51. "Part Four: Security Sector Reform, Article VII Disbandment of Irregular Forces, Reforming And Restructuring of the Liberian Armed Forces," in Comprehensive Peace Agreement Between the Government of Liberia and the Liberians United for Reconciliation and Democracy (LURD) and the Movement for Democracy in Liberia (MODEL) and Political Parties.

52. "USG Pre-Assessment Trip to Liberia on Security Sector Reform," Washington, DC: U.S. State Department, January 2004.

53. This definition is the author's.

54. Failed states and conflict-affected areas are settings of extreme poverty, lacking infrastructure, law, and security. Simply moving across the country can become a daunting expedition involving robust security convoys, careful route reconnaissance, resupply points, spare vehicles, air medical evacuation support, river-crossing capabilities, disciplined staff, and significant contingency planning. Other factors that affect operations include institutionalized corruption, exotic diseases, prevalent traffic accidents, lack of logistical resupply, wild animals, and high rates of crime. Even amenities such as potable water, electricity, and shelter cannot be assumed. Staff must be prepared for possible lack of cooperation from authorities, the novelty of the procedure for the population, absence of precedents, and cultural misunderstandings that could be disastrous. In light of this backdrop, DynCorp's achievements are all the more notable.

55. *Liberia: Uneven Progress in Security Sector Reform*, Africa Report No. 148, New York: International Crisis Group, 2009.

56. Offering no U.S. support for Liberia SSR was also considered, but dismissed. "USG Pre-Assessment Trip to Liberia on Security Sector Reform," Washington, DC: U.S. State Department, January 2004.

57. DynCorp International and MPRI are private security or military companies, while PA&E is focuses on construction work, specializing in conflict zone operations. At the time, PA&E personnel did not carry weapons or train others how to use them.

58. Robbers killed John Auffrey, a DoD civilian, in his room at the Mamba Point Hotel, Monrovia, on May 23, 2004. At the time, he was the security assistance program administrator at the U.S. Embassy in Namibia.

59. "New Armed Forces of Liberia Force Opt Working Brief," Paper presented at the SSR Assessment Mission, Monrovia, 2004.

60. It may also have something to do with the DoD's general aversion to all things African following the 1993 Somalia disaster.

61. Klein suggested that Liberia could make do with a decent police force and a well-trained border security force of 600 to 700 men. The actual statement was made on November 5, 2003. "Liberia: US Hires Private Company to Train 4,000-Man Army," IRIN Africa, Nairobi, Africa: Integrated Regional Information Networks, February 15, 2005. His opinion may have also been informed by UNMIL's civilian police (CIVPOL) commissioner, Mark Kroeker, who told U.S. State Department personnel that Liberia needed a robust police force and not a military. "USG Pre-Assessment Trip to Liberia on Security Sector Reform," Washington, DC: U.S. State Department, January 2004.

62. AFL mission statement taken from the CPA. See "Comprehensive Peace Agreement Between the Government of Liberia and the Liberians United for Reconciliation and Democracy (LURD) and the Movement for Democracy in Liberia (MODEL) and Political Parties," Part Four, Article VII, Para. 2.c.

63. For example, see Morten Bøås and Karianne Stig, "Security Sector Reform in Liberia: An Uneven Partnership Without Local Ownership," *Journal of Intervention and Statebuilding*, Vol. 4, No. 3, 2010, pp. 285-303; Adedeji Ebo, "Liberia Case Study: Outsourcing SSR to Foreign Companies," Laurie Nathan, ed., *No Ownership, No Commitment. A Guide to Local Ownership of Security Sector Reform*, Birmingham, UK: University of Birmingham, 2007; Mark Malan, "Security Sector Reform in Liberia: Mixed Results From Humble Beginnings," Carlisle, PA: Strategic Studies Institute, U.S. Army War College, 2008.

64. Carl von Clausewitz, *On War*, Princeton, NJ: Princeton University Press, 1976, p. 119. The original DoS plan specifies that training begin within 3 months of the contract award, meaning that basic training would commence in January 2005. In reality, the first basic training class started in July 2006.

65. National Transitional Government of Liberia, Executive Order No. 5: Demobilisation and Retirement of Soldiers, Monrovia, Liberia: National Transitional Government of Liberia, 2005; National Transitional Government of Liberia, AFL Restructuring Policy, Monrovia, Liberia: National Transitional Government of Liberia, 2005; Government of Liberia, Liberian National Defense Strategy (Draft), Monrovia, Liberia: National Transitional Government of Liberia, 2006.

66. T. E. Lawrence, *Seven Pillars of Wisdom*, London, UK: Wordsworth Editions, 1997.

67. This should not be confused with counterinsurgency (COIN) operations, which seek to provide short-term remedies to popular grievances long enough to establish control over an area. COIN is not sustainable development nor necessarily supports it.

68. True, the United States builds more than just conventional forces units. In recent years, the United States has helped partners develop counterterrorist special forces units, but these are primarily assault forces that do little to remedy the source of many internal threats: the failures of development, bad governance, and violent ideologies. These are threats that special forces units can repress, but not resolve.

69. UNDP, *Human Development Report 1994*, Oxford, UK: Oxford University Press, 1994, p. 2. See also Francis Mading Deng *et al.*, *Sovereignty as Responsibility: Conflict Management in Africa*, Washington, DC: Brookings Institution Press, 1996; Neil Macfarlane and Yuen Foong Khong, *Human Security and the UN: A Critical History*, Indianapolis, IN: Indiana University Press, 2006.

70. Government Of Liberia, Liberian National Defense Strategy (Draft).

71. National Transitional Government of Liberia, Executive Order No. 5.

72. Although DynCorp was not quite out of Liberia yet. In a new task order (worth $20 million if all options were exercised), DynCorp was selected to provide the AFL with operations and maintenance services. This task order was awarded under the new 5-year State Department Indefinite Delivery, Indefinite Quantity (IDIQ) contract called the Africa Peacekeeping Program (AFRICAP), contract solicitation number SAQMMA08R0237. Awardees under AFRICAP include DynCorp International, PA&E Government Services, AECOM, and Protection Strategies Incorporated.

73. *Liberia: Uneven Progress in Security Sector Reform*, p. 9.

74. Voice of America is the official external broadcast institution of the U.S. Federal Government. During the Cold War, Voice of America maintained a large facility in Liberia, but the facility was sacked during the Liberian Civil War.

75. In late April 2006, 400 to 500 former AFL soldiers conducted a violent protest outside the ministry and clashed with UNMIL peacekeepers sent to contain the unrest. They claimed nonpayment of salary arrears and retirement benefits and demanded back pay, which some reportedly received while others did not. See Ansorge and Antwi-Ansorge, "Monopoly, Legitimacy, Force"; "President Authorizes Defense Ministry to Pay Salary Arrears to Former Soldiers," UNMIL (media summary citing ELBS Radio and Star Radio), June 14, 2006; Brownie J. Samukai, Jr., "A Discussion with Liberia's Defense Minister, Brownie J. Samukai, Jr.," United States Institute of Peace, Washington, DC, May 11, 2007; "Leadership of Demobilized AFL Soldiers Assure

President Sirleaf of Unwavering Support," Executive Mansion, Press Release, February 24, 2010; Nicholas Cook, *Liberia's Post-War Development*, Washington, DC: Congressional Research Service, Footnote 75.

76. Ansorge and Antwi-Ansorge, "Monopoly, Legitimacy, Force."

77. The DAMC included representatives from the Executive Mansion, Ministry of National Defence, Ministry of Finance, Central Bank of Liberia, Ministry of Information, Ministry of Planning, U.S. Embassy, UN, Economic Community of West African States, the African Union, and the International Contact Group on Liberia. See National Transitional Government of Liberia, Executive Order No. 5, clause 3.

78. The criteria used to screen applicants were personal data (some fields in the database have no information); date of birth (DOB) versus date of entry (DOE) into the AFL (those with DOBs after 1973 were disqualified from joining the service, since AFL standards required rigid application of a minimum entry age of 17); DOE versus training base (the AFL had fixed official training bases, and some of them were not operational at certain times); whether the re-documentation form was personally filled in, as required by the process (questions were raised if another person did the writing for a lettered personnel); a cross-check with DDRR list from UNMIL resulting in "double dipping" (AFL personnel processed through the UNMIL DDRR program were excluded from the AFL demobolization process); a cross-check with the MOD insurance benefit list (no impersonation of dead service personnel); commander certification (each unit commander was required to review and certify the accuracy and completeness of the respective unit rosters under penalty of perjury and possible loss of all benefits and exclusion from possible re-entry consideration in the new AFL); and a photo check (all re-documented personnel had photo forms; there was a facial check at time of payment).

79. Each senior officer was chief of the following military staff offices: G1 (personnel), G3 (operations), G4 (logistics), adjutant general, engineers, chief information officer, signal, assistant G1, and brigade element.

80. National Transitional Government of Liberia-Ministry of Defense, Operation Order 001-Operation Demobilization, 2005.

81. The $15 million cost number comes from: Cook, Footnote 75.

82. For example, instead of saying "He bothers me," one would say "He vexes me," delivered in heavy patois. M. Paul Lewis, ed., *Ethnologue: Languages of the World*, 16th Ed., Dallas, TX: SIL International, 2009.

83. *Interagency Assessment of Iraq Police Training: Joint Inspector General Report*, Washington, DC: U.S. Department of State and Department of Defense, 2005, p. 22.

84. ICG, *Liberia: Uneven Progress in Security Sector Reform*. For more information on this vetting technique, see Sean McFate, "The Art and Aggravation of Vetting in Post-Conflict Environments," *Military Review*, July/August 2007, pp. 79-97.

85. DynCorp approached several organizations for vetting purposes. The government of Liberia, such that it was, provided limited information through its Ministry of Justice and Liberian National Police (for criminal records); Ministry of Education (for verification of education level and identity); Ministry of Health (for verification of date and place of birth, citizenship, and identity); Ministry of Defence (for prior record of service in the AFL, re-documentation exercise, surviving records, and demobilization exercise); and Ministry of Gender (for rape and other gender-related allegations). The UN and UNMIL's various agencies provided records regarding identity, human rights violation allegations and war crimes, child soldiers, witness testimony from IDP camps, criminal activity, and combatant demobilization lists. NGOs proved an excellent source on human rights violation allegations, and included international organizations such as the ICRC, ICG, IRC, and WAEC. Local NGOs also provided excellent information on human rights violation allegations and included the National Human Rights Centre of Liberia, National Human Rights Commission, National Association of Female Lawyers, Liberia National Law Enforcement Association, Methodists Human Rights Commission, and Catholic Justice and Peace Commission.

86. The tribal or ethnic groups are Kpelleh, Bassa, Gio, Kru, Grebo, Mano, Krahn, Gola, Gbandi, Loma, Kissi, Vai, Dei, Bella, Mandingo, Mende, and Sarpo.

87. However, this directive probably served political rather than operational purposes. By comparison, women comprise 14.5 percent of the U.S. military, 13 percent of the Australian Defence Force, and 9.6 percent of the UK armed forces. See "Statistics on Women in the [U.S.] Military," Arlington, VA: Women In Military Service For America Memorial Foundation, September 30, 2010, available from *www.womensmemorial.org/Press/stats.html*; *2005–06 Defence Annual Report*, Canberra, Australia: Australian Defence Force, 2006, p. 281; "Table 3a-Strength of UK Regular Forces By Sex," London, UK: UK Ministry of Defence, available from *www. dasa.mod.uk/applications/newWeb/www/apps/publications/pubView-File.php?content=170.131&date=2011-05-12&type=html&PublishTi me=09:30:00*.

88. Author interview, Monrovia, Liberia, June 5, 2006.

89. DynCorp's AFL basic training program was informed by the following U.S. Army training doctrine and best practices: the U.S. Army model of basic combat training (BCT), influenced by the U.S. Army's 1983 and 1985 study and subsequent reviews of the BCT program; U.S. Army Training and Doctrine Command, *TRADOC Regulation 350-6: Enlisted Initial Entry Training (IET) Policies and Administration*, Washington, DC: Headquarters, Department of the Army, 2003; and the U.S. Army's program of instruction for basic training at Ft. Jackson, SC. U.S. Army and AFL basic training relies on a three-phase "soldierization" process. Phase I plunges recruits into regimented army life and organizes them into 30-man platoons. Phase II continues the enforcement of standards and begins combat training, such as basic rifle marksmanship (BRM) and physical training, and creates a company mindset, whereby all rise or fall together. Phase III concentrates on individual tactical training, movement techniques, small unit tactics, map reading, land navigation, first aid, and other soldier skills. Transitioning from one phase to another was treated as a rite of passage as the training cadre evaluated and counseled each recruit regarding his or her performance and determined whether he or she should "recycle" the phase or advance to the next one. Basic training culminated with a tough field training exercise

(FTX) that, like a final exam, amalgamated all previous tactical training, plus a 20-kilometer forced march. If recruits passed, they graduated to Advanced Individual Training (AIT).

90. Some topics, such as civil disobedience, were omitted from the civics curriculum for obvious reasons.

91. For more on the challenges of ministerial transformation in SSR, see Elizabeth Panarelli, *The Role of the Ministerial Advisor in Security Sector Reform: Navigating Institutional Terrains*, Washington, DC: United States Institute of Peace, 2009; Robert M. Perito, *The Interior Ministry's Role in Security Sector Reform*, Washington, DC: United States Institute of Peace, 2009; Susanna Bearne, *National Security Decision-Making Structures and Security Sector Reform*, Cambridge, UK: Rand Europe, 2006.

92. DynCorp identified 10 functional areas for the Liberian MOD: operations; policy and plans; personnel and administration; resource management, fiscal acquisition/logistics; facilities; legal counsel; comptroller and budget planning; inspector general; protocol; and office administration.

93. At the time, much DoS peacekeeping operations (PKO) funding was being diverted to stem the worsening situation in Darfur among other priorities.

94. Total demobilization costs totalled approximately $15 million. Cook, p. 22.

95. Thomas Dempsey, *Security Sector Reform in Liberia Part I: An Assessment of Defense Reform*, Issue Paper No. 2008, Carlisle, PA: Peacekeeping and Stability Operations Institute, U.S. Army War College, 2008, p. 3.

96. Malan, p. x. See also Cook, p. 23.

97. Despite this growing consensus, ownership remains a contested concept, and how one translates this principle into practice is challenging. For more information on this topic, see Elizabeth Panarelli, *Local Ownership of Security Sector Reform*, Washington, DC, United States Institute for Peace, 2009; Marc J. Cohen and Tara R. Gingerich, *Protect and Serve or Train and Equip? U.S. Secu-*

rity Assistance and Protection of Civilians, Washington, DC: Oxfam America, 2009.

98. Nathan, p.1.

99. Ebo, "Liberia Case Study"; Bøås and Stig; Louise Andersen, *Post-Conflict Security Sector Reform and the Challenge of Ownership: The Case of Liberia*, Copenhagen, Denmark: Danish Institute for International Studies, 2006.

100. Bøås and Stig, p. 286.

101. Cook, p. 26.

102. Ebo, "Liberia Case Study," pp. 154-155.

103. Bøås and Stig.

104. *Ibid.*, p. 289.

105. *Ibid.* Other references cited include Ebo, "Liberia Case Study"; Adedeji Ebo, "The Challenges and Opportunities of Security Sector Reform in Post-Conflict Liberia," Occasional Paper No. 9, Geneva, Switzerland: Geneva Centre for Democratic Control of Armed Forces, 2005, pp. 1-28; Alexander Loden, "Civil Society and Security Sector Reform in Post-Conflict Liberia: Painting a Moving Train Without Brushes," *International Journal of Transitional Justice*, Vol. 1, No. 2, 2007, pp. 297-307.

106. *Status of Forces Agreement NTGL/MFA/0212/2-2/05: Arrangement Between the Government of the United States of America and the National Transitional Government of Liberia Concerning Security Sector Reform in the Republic of Liberia*, Monrovia, Liberia: Liberian Ministry of Foreign Affairs, 2005.

107. ICG, *Liberia: Uneven Progress in Security Sector Reform*, pp. i-ii.

108. Malan, p. 69.

109. Frances Z. Brown, "Bureaucracy Does Its Thing, Again," *The American Interest*, November/December, 2012, p. 46.

110. *Warlord, Inc.: Extortion and Corruption along the U.S. Supply Chain in Afghanistan: Report before the Subcommittee on National Security and Foreign Affairs*, Washington, DC: U.S. House of Representatives, 111th Cong., June 22, 2010, p. 2.

111. *Ibid.*

112. "The OSCE Strategic Police Matters Unit," Vienna, Austria: Organization for Security and Co-operation in Europe, October 3, 2008, available from *www.osce.org/spmu/13732*.

113. Robert M. Perito, *Afghanistan's Civil Order Police Victim of Its Own Success*, Washington, DC: United States Institute of Peace, 2012.

ANNEX

LIBERIA MILITARY PROGRAM TIMELINE

January 2003	DynCorp International (DynCorp) and Pacific Architects and Engineers (PA&E) are both awarded a State Department 5-year IDIQ contract to support peacekeeping and security efforts in Africa (contract solicitation number S-LMAQM-03-C-0034). Its minimum guaranteed expenditure is $5 million and maximum is $100 million, later expanded to $500 million.
August 2003	Charles Taylor flees Liberia, and 1,000 ECOWAS peacekeepers and 200 U.S. troops arrive. The interim government and rebels sign the CPA. Gyude Bryant is chosen to head the NTGL under the title "Chairman" rather than "President."
September–October 2003	U.S. forces pull out, and UNMIL begins the peacekeeping mission, deploying thousands of troops and encompassing the ECOWAS forces.
December 2003	UNMIL begins DDRR for rebel combatants only. AFL personnel are disarmed, but not demobilized, rehabilitated, and reintegrated. After riots at one DDRR site, UNMIL shuts down the program.
January 2004	U.S. sends a six-person SSR pre-assessment team to Liberia, January 21–29. The U.S. is responsible for the SSR of the AFL, as agreed to at Accra during peace talks. The DoS is the lead agency within the U.S. Government.
February 2004	International donors pledge more than $500 million in reconstruction aid to Liberia.
April 2004	UNMIL commences the DDRR process, and it continues without serious incident. UNMIL also begins SSR for civilian elements of the security sector, such as the Liberian national police. The DoS plans an SSR assessment mission to Liberia involving DoS, DoD, and contractors.
May 2004	DoS leads a 10-day assessment mission of SSR for the AFL. The team consists of experts drawn from DoS, DoD, and two contractor teams: DynCorp and PA&E. Additionally, PA&E subs MPRI because of its PMC expertise (PA&E is a GC firm whereas DynCorp and MPRI are PMCs with relevant SSR expertise). DDR of the AFL is not considered because the NTGL is responsible for this. A member of the assessment team is murdered in his hotel room while being robbed.
June 2004	DoD determines it cannot conduct the SSR program, and the DoS decides to outsource the SSR program entirely to the private sector. Accordingly, it asks both DynCorp and PA&E to submit their assessments and recommendations for SSR.

July 2004	After reviewing the assessments, DoS decides to divide SSR responsibilities between the two companies based on their expertise. DynCorp is responsible for reconstituting the AFL and MOD. PA&E is tasked with constructing most of the military bases and also providing specialty training, equipment, logistics, and base services.
September 2004	DoS tenders a task order RFP and SOW to DynCorp and PA&E entitled "Liberia Security Sector Reform." The SOW states that they must create a 2,000-person military, scalable to 4,300 personnel if funding permits, and an MOD.
October 2004	DynCorp and PA&E submit their proposals to DoS on October 7. DoS awards the task order to both companies with a division of labor as outlined in July. DynCorp is required to be on the ground initially, with PA&E to follow once sufficient units are fielded. Riots in Monrovia leave 16 people dead; UNMIL says former combatants and AFL veterans were behind the violence.
January 2005	DoS authorizes DynCorp to deploy a small planning team to Liberia to engage stakeholders and design the SSR program. It becomes clear that the NTGL lacks the capacity to conduct DDR of the AFL, and DoS asks DynCorp to take on this task. UNMIL imposes a curfew on several southeastern provinces owing to ritual human sacrifices and cannibalism, including the involvement of provincial governors.
February-March 2005	Consultations are held with major stakeholders regarding the mission and composition of the future AFL. This includes civil society, the standing AFL, former warring parties and political factions, UNMIL, the NTGL, civil society through the NTGL, and other entities. A comprehensive recruiting and vetting plan is devised intended to screen out human rights abusers from joining the AFL.
April 2005	The NTGL releases its AFL Restructuring Policy. Consultations with stakeholders continue. Topics include mission and force structure of the future AFL, location of training bases, sensitization campaign for civil society, and arrears owed unpaid AFL veterans.
May 2005	The demobilization plan is drafted and presented to Chairman Bryant. He signs Executive Order Number Five on May 15, authorizing the full demobilization of all legacy AFL units as of June 30, 2005. The DoS issues DynCorp a formal task order for the demobilization of the AFL, releasing full payment to the contractor. DynCorp makes preparations for DDR operations outside of Monrovia and plans to conduct the demobilization, recruiting staff both locally and internationally, and builds up its program (and presence) in Liberia. PA&E is to begin its portion of the program once training commences.

July 2005	DynCorp builds a demobilization site outside Monrovia. The demobilization and reintegration of the legacy soldiers commences. The U.S. Government approves DynCorp's blueprint for the new AFL's force structure and TO&E in Washington, DC. Construction of AFL training facilities starts but is slowed by the heavy rainy season.
September 2005	The NTGL agrees to allow the international community to supervise its finances in an effort to reduce corruption.
October 2005	Recruiting and vetting for the new AFL begins. Over 12,000 applicants will be processed in the next 2 years.
November 2005	Ellen Johnson-Sirleaf becomes the first woman to be elected as an African head of state. She takes office the following January.
December 2005	Construction of the new training base remains suspended as Liberia, the United States, and UNMIL debate over its location, costing the program money and time.
January 2006	DDR of 13,770 AFL soldiers is completed. Recruiting and vetting begins at the Barclay Training Center (BTC) in downtown Monrovia. Johnson-Sirleaf is sworn in as President, and the NTGL is abolished. Brownie Samukai replaces Daniel Chea as Liberian Minister of Defence.
February 2006	The demobilization of the AFL is successfully completed, perhaps the first time in modern African history that an entire standing military was safely demobilized without significant incident.
March 2006	Johnson-Sirleaf calls for Nigeria to hand over Taylor, which it does. Upon his arrival in Monrovia, he is transferred to the custody of UNMIL and immediately flown to Sierra Leone to stand trial before the UN-backed Sierra Leone Special Court on charges of crimes against humanity.
April 2006	MOD transformation begins at BTC. Approximately 400–500 former AFL soldiers conduct a violent protest outside the MOD, claiming nonpayment of salary arrears and retirement benefits, and clash with UNMIL peacekeepers sent to contain the unrest. Taylor appears before the Sierra Leone Special Court.
May 2006	Samukai spends a week in Washington, DC, with the DoS, DoD, and DynCorp to discuss the progress of SSR and formulation of the Liberian National Defence Strategy.

June 2006	DoS issues an updated SOW. DynCorp assists the MOD in a first draft of the national defense strategy. It is written based on the concept of human security, seeking to align the AFL's mission with the goals of development for durable stability and security. Progress is limited because the NTGL, UNMIL, the United States, and others are delayed with the national security strategy. The UN Security Council eases a ban on weapons sales so that Liberia can import small arms for government purposes only. An embargo on Liberian timber exports is lifted shortly afterward. A TRC is set up to investigate human rights abuses between 1979 and 2003. Tensions transpire between the TRC and SSR program as the TRC requests access to SSR vetting records, but the SSR team denies this request since it might compromise sources and methods, possibly resulting in reprisal killings of victims who spoke to the SSR vetting team on condition of anonymity about human rights abuses of some AFL candidates. The ICC at The Hague agrees to host Taylor's trial.
July 2006	The first class of AFL basic training or IET begins at BTC. It comprises 110 candidates, most of whom are selected for their potential to fill the leadership ranks first. The former U.S. Voice of America transmitter site is finally selected as the AFL's main training base, located at Careysburg and rechristened the Sandee S. Ware Military Barracks. DynCorp begins construction once the occupying UNMIL units move offsite. Construction is slowed by the heavy rainy season. DynCorp begins the process of purchasing and importing arms into Liberia for the AFL. President Johnson-Sirleaf switches on generator-powered street lights in the capital, which has been without electricity for 15 years.
August 2006	DynCorp orchestrates the first major shipment of arms, which arrives at Monrovia for the AFL. It is the first legal shipment in over 15 years.
November 2006	The first AFL basic training class of 102 graduates. AFL training of future classes is halted owing to U.S. funding shortfalls.
March 2007	119 civilian MOD employees graduate from a 17-week SSR program training course. Following this, the MOD reform program is prematurely terminated because of U.S. funding shortfalls.
April 2007	The UN Security Council votes to lift its ban on Liberian diamond exports. The ban was imposed in 2001 to stem the flow of blood diamonds, which helped fund the civil war.
May 2007	The UN urges Liberia to outlaw trial by ordeal.
June 2007	Taylor's war crimes trial begins at The Hague, where he stands accused of instigating atrocities in Sierra Leone.
September 2007	639 total personnel are trained. Owing to cost overruns, DoS shortens IET from 11 weeks to 8 weeks by cutting 3 weeks that were devoted to human rights, civics, and laws of war training.

January 2008	1,124 total personnel are trained.
April 2008	1,634 total personnel are trained.
September 2008	2,113 total personnel are trained.
January–December 2009	PA&E conducts unit training for the battalions, culminating in an ARTEP.
December 2009	The TRC releases its final report.
January 2010	DynCorp's and PA&E's contract for SSR ends, and a team of 60 U.S. Marines begin a 5-year mentorship program with the AFL in Operation ONWARD LIBERTY. In a new task order (worth $20 million if all options are exercised), DynCorp is selected to provide the AFL with operations and maintenance services. This task order is awarded under the new 5-year DoS IDIQ contract called the Africa Peacekeeping Program (AFRICAP), contract solicitation number SAQMMA08R0237. Awardees under AFRICAP include DynCorp International, PA&E Government Services, AECOM, and Protection Strategies Incorporated.